The POWER Series

TANK ATTACK

A Primer of Modern Tank Warfare

Steven J. Zaloga and Michael Green

Motorbooks International
Publishers & Wholesalers

First published in 1991 by Motorbooks International
Publishers & Wholesalers, P O Box 2, 729 Prospect
Avenue, Osceola, WI 54020 USA

The information in this book is true and complete to
the best of our knowledge. All recommendations are
made without any guarantee on the part of the author
or publisher, who also disclaim any liability incurred in
connection with the use of this data or specific details

Motorbooks International recommends you follow all
safety procedures when working on your vehicle. Wear
eye protection and a respiration filter, especially when
painting and around tools. Always dispose of
hazardous fluids, batteries, tires and parts properly and
safely to protect our environment

We recognize that some words, model names and
designations, for example, mentioned herein are the
property of the trademark holder. We use them for
identification purposes only. This is not an official
publication

Motorbooks International books are also available at
discounts in bulk quantity for industrial or sales-
promotional use. For details write to Special Sales
Manager at the Publisher's address

Library of Congress Cataloging-in-Publication Data
Zaloga, Steve.
    Tank attack / Steven J. Zaloga ; photo editor,
Michael Green.
      p. cm. — (The Power series)
    ISBN 0-87938-535-9
    1. Tank warfare.   I. Title.   II. Series;
Power series (Osceola, Wis.)
UG446.5.Z332   1991
358'.18—dc20   90-37728

Printed and bound in Hong Kong

On the front cover: *An M1 Abrams main battle
tank charges forward during exercises at the U.S.
National Training Center in the Mojave desert. The
combat capability of a tank is not simply the hardware, but the rigorous training of its crew as well.*
Greg Stewart

On the title page: *A pair of U.S. 7th Army M1A1
Abrams main battle tanks sit menacingly on the
fields of Germany during peacetime exercises. Only
a few years later these tanks would be showing their
combat capabilities in Iraq and Kuwait.* Michael
Green

On the frontispiece: *An unlikely location for a tank?
Not really. Modern tanks must be prepared to
operate from the chilly latitudes of the arctic, to the
scorching sun of the desert, to the fetid swamps of
the jungles. Fording a river is just another day's
work for the XM4 AGS (Armored Gun System), a
light tank privately developed by FMC Corp. to
satisfy U.S. Army requirements for an air-mobile
vehicle suitable for rapid deployment forces.* Huck
Hagenbuch/FMC Corp.

On the back cover: *Above, the M1A1's closest contemporary, the German Leopard II. Below, M1A1s
on maneuvers in Germany.* Michael Green

Contents

Acknowledgments

A dawn tank attack by the vaunted OPFOR—the enemy forces used during peacetime wargames at the U.S. Army's National Training Center. Their tanks are modified M551 Sheridans. Steven Zaloga

The preparation of a book like this takes extensive cooperation from the United States Army. The majority of the photos have been taken at over a dozen army bases around the world. We would especially like to thank the public affairs offices at Ft. Hood, Ft. Knox, and Aberdeen Proving Grounds. Special thanks also to Greg Stewart, Dave Appel, Albert Davis, and Michael Mitalek for their contributions to this book.

The author would also like to thank many friends and tankers who read the manuscript and offered helpful comments and corrections. Thanks go to Russ Vaughn, Cookie Sewell, Brian Gibbs, Doug MacGregor, and many others who shared their experiences serving in armor units. Thanks also go to Lon Nordeen and Jim Loop for their help on this project.

Glossary

APC Armored personnel carrier, an infantry transporter such as the M113. More sophisticated infantry transporters with turreted weapon systems are called IFVs.

APFSDS Armor-piercing, fin-stabilized, discarding-sabot. Popularly called a ''sabot'' round. The standard type of kinetic energy penetrator ammunition used in tank fighting. The round resembles a long dart, with a sabot in the middle to match the bore diameter.

Battalion Standard tactical formation, consisting of several companies. Several battalions form a regiment. American armor battalions today typically have 50-plus tanks, while a typical Soviet tank battalion has over 30. Actual tank strengths in a battalion have varied through history and are fixed by the current Tables of Organization and Equipment (TO&E).

BMP Russian acronym for infantry fighting vehicle. The Soviet equivalent of the U.S. Army's M2 Bradley IFV.

Boresight To adjust the main gun of the tank so that the sights and gun tube are properly aligned.

Brew up Traditional expression (originally British) for a catastrophic internal tank fire.

BRL Ballistics Research Laboratory, located at Aberdeen Proving Ground in Maryland. An element of the U.S. Army's research and development sector, where research on advanced tank armor and tank munitions is undertaken.

Cadillacs American tankers' slang for the gunner's hand controls. It stems from the manufacturer of tank stabilization equipment, Cadillac-Gage.

Caliber The diameter of a gun or cannon tube. So ''105mm gun'' refers to a tank gun with a bore diameter of 105mm.

CAT Canadian Army Trophy. A periodic tank gunnery competition staged in Germany, involving most NATO armies.

Chobham armor A type of advanced laminate armor using steel, special metal baffles, and other materials. Designed in Britain in the 1970s, this armor is used in new NATO tanks such as the Challenger, M1 Abrams, and Leopard II. Also called Burlington armor.

Company A standard tactical formation, consisting of several platoons. Several companies form a battalion.

Cupola A traversable sub-turret or hatch element mounted on the roof of a tank turret.

CVC Combat vehicle crewman. Slang for the helmet worn by American tankers.

CWS Commander's weapon station. The cupola and machine gun station for the tank commander in the M1 Abrams.

Depleted uranium A type of uranium metal used in the manufacture of tank projectiles and special armors. The metal comes from spent (depleted radiation) uranium nuclear powerplant fuel.

ERA Explosive reactive armor.

FLIR Forward-looking infrared. A weapon sight that detects a target by sensing the minute temperature difference between a man-made object, such as a tank, and the cooler natural background. Also called a thermal imaging sight.

4-68 Armor 4th Battalion, 68th Armored Regiment. Example of the standard U.S. Army fashion for designating the subcomponents of tactical formations.

Glacis plate The sloping front plate of a tank hull.

GPS Gunner's primary sight. This sighting system in the M1 Abrams is linked to the electro-optical FLIR sight, computer, and laser rangefinder. The auxiliary sight, basically a simple telescopic sight, is used if the GPS fails.

HEAT High-explosive antitank. A type of antitank warhead using a shaped charge (hollow charge), chemical energy warhead.

Hull down Tankers' slang for a stationary tank hidden by terrain features or entrenchments with only the turret exposed. This is the ideal defensive position for a tank since the earth protects a large portion of the tank.

IMP1 Improved Product M1 (Abrams tank). An interim version of the Abrams tank, with the same 105mm gun system of the M1 variant, but the improved armor package and other features of the later M1A1 tank.

KE Kinetic energy. Tank projectiles that penetrate armor by means of the speed and mass of the projectile, not by explosive (chemical) energy.

Klick U.S. Army slang for ''kilometer.''

M Prefix for U.S. Army ordnance designations, such as M1 tank. Traditionally, the designation was written with a dash separating the sequential number, such as M-4 Sherman tank. Since the 1970s, the U.S. Army has officially deleted the dash on newer equipment, so M1 Abrams rather than M-1 Abrams tank. The suffix indicates later models of the weapon. So M2 is the initial version, M2A1 the second version, M2A2 the third version, etc.

M2 Bradley IFV Current U.S. Army infantry fighting vehicle used by the mechanized infantry. The armored cavalry version is the M3 CFV.

Mantlet The protective armor cover attached to the gun which elevates and depresses along with the main armament.

Platoon Standard small unit tactical formation. A typical American tank platoon today is four tanks, while a Soviet tank platoon has three tanks. Several platoons form a company.

Reactive armor A protective system for tanks, mounted over the existing steel armor. The standard type, called explosive reactive armor, degrades the impact of a shaped-charge warhead by hurling a disruptor plate by explosive force into the path of the warhead blast.

RPG-7 Widely used Soviet-designed rocket-propelled antitank grenade which entered service in the 1960s. Carried by a single infantryman, it can penetrate about 280mm (11 inches) of steel armor. It is being replaced in the Soviet Army by the improved RPG-16.

Sabot American tanker's slang for APFSDS tank ammunition; pronounced sā-bō, without the t. Sabot refers to the metal or plastic sleeve around the sub-caliber dart projectile which permits the narrow dart to travel down the wider gun tube. Once the projectile exits the gun tube, the sabot falls off.

Shaped charge A type of missile or tank projectile warhead that penetrates armor by using a directed high explosive blast. It is called shaped charge since the explosive is shaped over a thin metal cone, usually made of copper.

Shot trap A weakness in the contour of a tank's armor which makes it more susceptible to penetration by an enemy weapon.

Sitrep Situation report.

Staballoy Euphemism for depleted uranium.

TC Tank commander.

Thermal imaging Another name for a FLIR sight. Electro-optical sighting device used on tanks and other weapons.

Zulu time The U.S. Army expression for Greenwich Mean Time.

Introduction

Operation Desert Storm has focused new attention on the role of tank forces in modern warfare. This book is intended to serve as a basic primer on the technology of modern tank warfare.

Tank warfare at one time was confined to the industrialized states of Europe and America. Tank forces outside of this region, even as late as World War II, were quite small. But today, nearly every army has a tank force of some size, and the tank force of some Third World countries like Iraq (at least before Desert Storm) outnumbered the tank forces of major European armies such as France, Germany, or Britain.

Tanks are the shock force of modern land armies. When it was time to launch the ground offensive against Iraq in February 1991, it was the tank and mechanized divisions which spearheaded the attack. The value of tank forces in modern warfare rests on three qualities—their firepower, their mobility, and their protective armor. Other forces possess one or more of these virtues. Artillery certainly matches the tank in firepower, but it lacks the tank's mobility and protection. Air mobile forces such as paratroopers and heliborne infantry surpass the tank in tactical and operational mobility, but they lack the tank's firepower and protection. Infantry, dug in behind a protective barrier of berms, trenches, and minefields like the Iraqi forces in Kuwait, match the tank in protection, but it lacks the tank's battlefield mobility.

Many technologies have been developed to sap the tank's strength. Modern anti-tank guided missiles have challenged the tank's heavy armor, and modern scatterable mines challenge the tank's mobility. But to date, no other weapon system offers a battlefield commander the destructive power of tanks.

This does not mean that tanks can dominate the battlefield without the aid of the other army branches or the other services. To the contrary, the tank depends on the other branches—infantry, artillery, engineer, aviation—to accentuate its virtues and minimize its weaknesses. When tank forces have been given undue predominance, as in the case of the Israeli force in 1973, the results can be tragic. But as Desert Storm has demonstrated, the tank, used as a central element in a combined arms force, still remains an essential tool in modern land warfare.

Chapter 1

Legacy

"Tanks have no future!" Skeptics have been saying that for years. In the 1920s, when a .50-caliber machine gun was a serious tank killer, critics said that the tank could not survive on the modern battlefield. World War II proved them wrong. Latter-day Cassandras said that the invention of guided antitank missiles sounded the death knell of the tank. Yet all modern armies are still based on tanks.

Tanks seem so anachronistic, like cast-iron relics of the Victorian age of industrialism. In an age of sleek F-14 Tomcat jet fighters and precision-guided missiles, the tank's crude finish and mud-splashed hide hints of an antediluvian ancestry. Their hulking mass conveys primeval menace. The idea of spending three million dollars for one of these brutish dinosaurs seems preposterous to many taxpayers. Yet the tank remains unchallenged as the centerpiece of all modern armies. In spite of its seeming crudity, the modern main battle tank is a sophisticated feat of engineering. It is as far removed from the World War II tank as today's modern jet fighter is from its propeller-driven antecedents.

Today's tank is an evolutionary outcome of profound changes on the twentieth-century battlefield. For centuries, land warfare revolved around a handful of basic combat arms. Artillery provided firepower. Horse cavalry provided mobility. Fortifications provided defensive protection. The tank blends these functions into a single piece of ordnance. It is this unique combination of features that makes the tank so versatile a weapon.

The tank's origins lie in the four hellish years of trench fighting of World War I. In a few short decades

A hint of the future. The first American tank battalions to see combat in World War I were commanded by this young Army colonel, George S. Patton, Jr. Patton's experience with the tanks in France in 1918 prompted his enthusiastic interest in mechanized warfare even through the lean interwar years of the 1920s and 1930s. The tank is a French Renault FT, the most modern type of the war. National Archives

at the end of the nineteenth century, the Industrial Revolution infected the military sphere. Warfare itself became industrialized. Never before had there been so rapid a rise in the killing power of weapons. Technical improvements in artillery made them far more efficient mass killers. Breech-loaded howitzers were many times more lethal than the crude bore-loaded guns in use since the Middle Ages. Howitzers could fire much more quickly, and their projectiles were crammed with the latest in industrial chemistry: new high explosives and chemical agents. Railroads and trucks kept the artillery amply supplied with their death-dealing munitions. The pace of development in small arms was every bit as frantic. Efficient bolt-action rifles more than quadrupled the firepower of the foot soldier. The rifle's close relative, the belt-fed machine gun, added to the slaughter.

The weapons had changed, but the soldier had not. The infantryman and cavalryman of 1914 were no better protected than one of Napoleon's soldiers a century before. Horse cavalry disappeared from the battlefield in the face of machine guns and modern artillery. Against such overwhelming firepower, infantry attacks on prepared positions became virtually suicidal. The infantry had no recourse but to burrow into the earth to seek protection. The impact of technology had been unanticipated by the military leaders, and most proved intellectually incapable of adapting to the change of tide.

A handful of imaginative officers quickly appreciated that the best antidote to the new firepower technology was other new technology—the armored vehicle. Armored vehicles would protect the soldier from the dire consequences of artillery and machine gun fire.

U.S. Army tanks were neglected in the 1920s and 1930s due to lack of money. Up until the late 1930s, the only tanks available in quantity were these arthritic old Six-Ton Tanks, an American copy of the French Renault FT–17 tank. **via Michael Green**

It would replace the mobility of the horse with the mobility of the motor. And it would defeat the machine gun nest with a bristling array of its own weapons.

We often forget that in the early days there was no consensus on how these armored vehicles would be configured. Early armored vehicles came in many shapes and sizes—cars, trains, and tanks. In some theaters, such as Russia, the armored train and armored car were the principal new weapons of mobile warfare. But on the western front, it was the tank. In the ensuing decades, the tank was perfected in both a technical and a tactical sense, and other forms of armored vehicles faded into obscurity.

In hindsight, it is easy to see how invaluable the tank would become in ending the stalemate of trench warfare. It is easy to scoff at the dunderheads who resisted the use of tanks. But early tanks were very flawed weapons. They were plagued with technical problems. Tanks were horribly unreliable. It was a major accomplishment to keep them operating for a few hours, to say nothing of actually performing combat missions. World War I tanks often had ranges of less than twenty-five miles. Refueling them on the battlefield was a real challenge, since the ground was chewed up by artillery fire and ordinary fuel trucks could not reach them.

Nor was it immediately apparent how to best use tanks on the battlefield. Should they fight alone, or should they be supported by infantry? Was artillery support a help or a hindrance? These questions were answered only by bloody experimentation in the final months of World War I and the opening years of World War II.

The tank's place on the battlefield was established during World War II. Tanks are synonymous with blitzkrieg. Unlike the bloody stalemate of trench warfare in 1914–18, World War II in Europe was a war of maneuver. Tanks formed the sharp end of the sword. When we recall many of the most famous campaigns—North Africa, Stalingrad, Kursk, the Battle of the Bulge—the tank springs immediately to mind. Even in theaters where the terrain did not favor massed tank formations—Italy, the Pacific islands,

Burma—tanks played an important infantry support role.

In the half century since World War II, tanks have often figured in the newspaper headlines. North Korean tanks spearheaded the 1950 invasion of South Korea. The 1956 Sinai war saw the coming of age of the legendary Israeli armored force. The clash between India and Pakistan over Kashmir in 1965 saw massive armored confrontations. The two largest wars in the Mideast, in 1967 and again in 1973, were primarily mechanized conflicts. Both the Iranians and the Iraqis made extensive use of tanks during the savage gulf war in the early 1980s. The bitter fighting

General George Patton again, this time as the head of one of the most formidable armored force ever amassed by the U.S. Army, the 3rd Army. Seen here in Germany in April 1945, Patton has reprimanded the soldiers of the M4A3 tank behind him for adding extra protective sandbags to their tank. Patton felt such improvisations showed a lack of confidence in American tanks and led to premature vehicle breakdowns. The tankers, appalled by the thin armor of the M4 Sherman tank, didn't agree and in typical GI fashion, ignored Patton's orders on the matter. U.S. Army/DoD

13

in Angola between South African and Cuban forces in 1986–88 saw extensive armored clashes. And of course, tanks were a central element in the ground phase of Operation Desert Storm. Tanks did not play a central role in the guerrilla wars in Algeria, Indochina, Vietnam, and Cambodia, but even in these wars, tanks were still present.

Tanks have become a ubiquitous element in nearly all land forces. Even the smallest Third World armies have a few companies of tanks. The utility of tanks in warfare is so widely recognized that many Third World countries—Brazil, India, Iraq, and North Korea—manufacture their own tanks.

But the pacesetters in tank design remain a handful of the major industrial powers in Europe and America. The confrontation between NATO and the Warsaw Pact has determined the pace of tank design over the past few decades, although certainly the lessons of the Mideast wars have not been ignored. This book looks at tanks primarily from the American perspec-

The pace of tank technology in World War II was not set in the West, but on the Eastern Front where the main tank battles were waged. The tank that set the standards for all future World War II tanks was the Soviet T–34, first seen in combat in 1941.

This particular tank is a T–34–85 manufactured in Czechoslovakia which served in the Egyptian Army in the 1967 and 1973 wars before being captured by the Israelis. It is now being used to train U.S. troops in vehicle recognition. Michael Green

U.S. tank designs in World War II such as this M4A3 Sherman were undergunned and underarmored, a sad reflection of the neglect of tank design before the war. But the American tanks had two advantages: there were more of them, and they were far more reliable and durable than their German opponents. The sandbags added to the tank were intended to protect the crew from German antitank rocket launchers. U.S. Army/DoD

tive. One might argue whether or not the United States builds the best tanks in NATO. But the United States does build the largest number of tanks of any NATO country, and their widespread export has made American designs influential around the world.

One reason for the sorry state of American tanks in World War II were the tank destroyers. Essentially lightly armored tanks with big guns, they diverted the best antitank weapons away from the tanks. The idea was a complete failure, and tank destroyers were abandoned by the U.S. Army after the war. U.S. Army/DoD

THE AMERICAN EXPERIENCE

The United States was a relative latecomer to the tank business. The first significant American tank, the Six-Ton Tank, was a license-produced copy of the revolutionary French Renault FT. It arrived in France too late to see fighting in World War I. At the same time, small numbers of the first indigenous American design, the Ford Three-Ton Tank, were also manufactured. This was a truly dreadful little death trap, and it was unceremoniously retired from service shortly after the war. American tank units in France used French or British tanks in combat. The World War I Tank Corps had an interesting influence two decades later. The commander of the largest tank units was a relatively obscure young colonel, George S. Patton, Jr. And his colleague in Pennsylvania in charge of training new tankers was an equally obscure young colonel, Dwight Eisenhower. The Tank Corps was dissolved after the war, but Patton's fascination with tanks endured.

Between the wars, the U.S. Army's interest in tanks languished. The staple of American tank battalions through the 1930s was the obsolete Six-Ton Tank. Americans were determined to avoid entanglement in another European war. Tanks seemed irrelevant to traditional army missions, such as patrolling the Mexican border or policing overseas colonies, such as the Philippines. Tank development was further complicated by internal army politics. Tanks were a political football between the infantry and cavalry branches, with the small research budget wasted between two competing sets of designs. By 1939, when war broke out again in Europe, the American tank force was on par with that of Poland and Italy and not at all comparable to that of France, Britain, and Germany.

In spite of widespread public reluctance to become involved in another European land war, most astute military leaders realized that the United States would be dragged into the war eventually. From 1939 to 1941, there was a furious effort to modernize the U.S. Army. Although American tank designs of the 1930s were unimpressive compared to their European counterparts, the army could count on a large and vigorous automotive and railroad industry. America rapidly went from being one of the smallest armored vehicle–producing countries to the largest. American designs weren't the best, but they were better than nothing. Through the Lend-Lease Act of 1941, they helped sustain the British army during the desert fighting in North Africa, and they even saw service in the Red Army on the Eastern Front.

Lacking experience in tank design and tank warfare, America turned to Britain for advice. The British army was in the forefront of army mechanization in the early 1930s and had extensive experience in tank fighting from the campaigns in North Africa. Although British influence was vital in the development of the infant U.S. Armored Force, there were drawbacks. Tank technology in World War II was pushed along by developments on the Eastern Front between Germany and the Soviet Union. The Germans were by far the most experienced practitioners of tank warfare during the war, and their best units were committed to the Eastern Front. Soviet technological innovations, especially the combat debut of their revolutionary T-34 tank in 1941, led to a fevered technological arms race in the East. Soviet innovations would be matched by German countermeasures, to be met with yet another Soviet innovation. This contest was largely invisible to American tank designers, their vision

The Korean War found the U.S. Army in a sorry shape again so far as tanks were concerned. After stunning defeats at the hands of North Korean T–34–85 tanks in the summer of 1950, the Army rushed better tanks to Korea, like these M–46 tanks near Yangpung in March 1951. The bright tiger markings painted on the tanks were supposed to terrify the superstitious Chinese troops; one suspects the very potent 90mm gun on the M–46 did a far better job of intimidation. U.S. Army/DoD

17

clouded by the British experiences. Unfortunately, British experience was obtained in North Africa. The Afrika Korps is legendary to western military historians but was a minor sideshow as far as the Germans were concerned. It did not compare to the titanic struggles on the Russian front. North Africa did not receive high priority for either the best men or the best equipment.

This was not very evident to American military leaders in 1943 when U.S. armored divisions received

Vietnam was hardly the best environment for tank warfare, but tanks served there as well. Vietnam was typical of many of the small wars in the Third World over the past few decades, where small numbers of *tanks are used mainly for infantry support. This U.S. Army M-48A3 Patton tank is on road patrol near Chu Chi in January 1969. U.S. Army/DoD*

their baptism of fire in North Africa. American tanks of the period, the M-3 and M-5 Stuart light tanks, and medium tanks such as the M-3 Lee and M-4 Sherman, were not outclassed by their German counterparts in Tunisia. They were often outfought by their more experienced German rivals, most embarrassingly so at the Kasserine Pass debacle. But this was to be expected in the first contest of an unblooded combat unit. The U.S. Army remained confident that its M-4 Sherman tank could stand on its own with its German rivals. Even the arrival of Tiger heavy tanks in Tunisia, and later Sicily, did not seriously undermine this unfortunate American overconfidence.

American tank designs were further hampered by a seriously flawed concept of tank fighting. American military leaders, led by Maj. Gen. Lesley McNair, viewed tanks as a weapon of exploitation. Two distinct types of armored vehicles were built: tanks and tank destroyers. The business of tanks was to exploit the breakthrough. The business of tank killing was to be left to the specialized Tank Destroyer branch. As a result, American tanks were given smaller guns than might otherwise have been the case. And the tank destroyers, given effective antitank guns, were too thinly armored to have the battlefield utility of true tanks.

By the time the U.S. armored force entered combat in the main theater in the summer of 1944, its tanks were hopelessly outclassed. The mainstay of the U.S. tank force was the M-4 Sherman, armed with a 75mm

Besides main battle tanks, the U.S. Army has also deployed light tanks for scouting and cavalry roles. The M-551 Sheridan first saw action in Vietnam. But its revolutionary missile-gun system proved *troublesome, and only a single battalion of these tanks remain in U.S. Army service, with the 82nd Airborne Division.* U.S. Army/DoD

gun. The Ordnance Department had developed an improved tank gun, the 76mm gun, for the M-4 medium tank. But even George Patton, usually an enthusiastic supporter of bigger guns, was reluctant to accept the new weapon for armored divisions under his command. The new M-26 Pershing heavy tank was being developed at an excruciatingly slow pace, and there was little demand for such a big tank from

the troops in the field. That is, until American tankers met the German Panther tank.

The Germans, shocked by the arrival of the Soviet T-34 tank in 1941, were determined to develop a superior tank. The Tiger I was fielded at the end of 1942 but was too clumsy and expensive to be adopted as a standard tank. It could supplement medium tanks but never replace them. The Panther would be the

The conflict which most heavily shaped Western thinking about tank warfare was the 1973 war between Israel, Syria and Egypt. Israeli tank forces, though outnumbered, were able to overcome Soviet-equipped Arab forces by superior crew training *and better tactics. American-manufactured M60A1 tanks were the standard type used by the Israelis in the Sinai desert fighting.* Israeli Government Press Agency

new medium tank. It was first sent into action at the great tank battle of Kursk-Orel on the Eastern Front in the summer of 1943. It could do little to stem the Soviet tide, being available in very small numbers and with serious mechanical bugs. American intelligence was vaguely aware of the Panther from liaison teams in the Soviet Union. As in the case of the Tiger I, which had been encountered in Tunisia and Sicily, the U.S. Army presumed that the Panther would never be available beyond a few independent tank regiments. Unfortunately, by the time of the Normandy invasion in 1944, the Panther made up half of the German tank force in France.

A duel between an M-4 Sherman and a Panther was a hopelessly uneven match. The short 75mm gun of the M-4 Sherman was incapable of penetrating the front armor of the Panther at normal combat ranges. The Panther, even though nearly twenty tons heavier, was more mobile over soft ground due to its wide tracks. And its long 75mm gun could gut a Sherman at any combat range. The only Sherman capable of dealing with the Panther was the Sherman Firefly. This was a British innovation that substituted the new 17-pounder antitank gun for the normal 75mm gun. It was available in very small numbers. The Panther caused an unpleasant shock for U.S. tankers in France. American soldiers had become accustomed to expecting the best weapons—the best rifles, the best machine guns, the best fighter planes. Sometimes their weapons were no better than German weapons but at least equal, and there were usually more of them. In the case of tanks, they were clearly inferior. Nor did the tank destroyers do much good. American soldiers complained bitterly that what was needed was "not a tank killer, but a killer tank."

The technological advantages enjoyed by the German panzer forces in France were not successful in affecting the outcome of the summer fighting. The panzers may have been tough-skinned beasts, but their numerous supporting trucks were not. The critical logistical system that fed the panzer divisions was pulverized by Allied fighter bombers. A Panther tank with no fuel or ammunition was just a heap of useless steel scrap. The quality of German troops was declin-

ing as well. The proud panzer veterans of Stalingrad, Tunisia, and Kursk were spread very thin among many green tank troops who hadn't received as much training as their American or British counterparts.

A single forgotten battle in September 1944 makes this clear. Near the village of Arracourt, elements of the U.S. 4th Armored Division ran head-on into a fresh Panther brigade. The numbers on both sides were fairly similar, and the Germans had a distinct technological edge. But after three months of hard fighting, the Americans were skilled veterans facing a green opponent. The Panther brigade was smashed in close-range fighting, where the Panther's advantages made no difference. Arracourt has been long since forgotten, even though it was one of the largest tank-vs-tank battles involving U.S. forces in 1944 until the Battle of the Bulge. It is worth remembering for two reasons. It highlights an often forgotten combat lesson: Experienced tankers in mediocre tanks will defeat better tanks in the hands of mediocre crews. Arracourt is also worth remembering for the man who led the 37th Tank Battalion at the center of the fight: Maj. Creighton Abrams. His name will appear often in this book.

The U.S. Army never secured technological superiority in tank combat with the German Wehrmacht. By 1945, it didn't matter. German tanks were seldom encountered. Panzer units were starved for fuel and often immobile. The panzer factories were pulverized by aerial bombardment. The main enemy became the tank hunters: carefully camouflaged antitank guns with the fine 75mm PaK 40, and teams of German infantry with the deadly little *panzerfaust* antitank rocket launchers.

After the Battle of the Bulge, there were no more massive tank duels. But many tankers remained haunted by memories of the summer of '44. Memories of 75mm rounds bouncing off the thick hides of Panthers. Memories of burned and blasted Sherman tanks in the hedgerows of Normandy. Memories of the sight and smell of a panzerfaust rocket burning through the Sherman's thin armor into the vulnerable insides of the tank.

Previous page
American tanks from 1945 to 1975 were based around evolutionary improvements in the M-26 Pershing tank. The final member of this family, the M60 series first entered service in 1960 and is still widely used by the U.S. Army and the U.S. Marine Corps. Shown is a heavily camouflaged M60A1 at Camp Roberts, California. Michael Green

The tankers vowed that never again would they fight in such inferior tanks. But memories fade with the contentment of peace, and by the late 1940s, tank design slid lower and lower on the list of American defense priorities. A brutish little war in a forgotten corner of the globe revived the old nightmares. In the summer of 1950, the North Korean Army, spearheaded by Soviet-manufactured T-34-85 tanks, sliced deep into South Korea and captured the capital of Seoul. American infantry battalions, equipped with outdated World War II bazooka antitank rocket launchers, were powerless to stop the tank attacks. Some infantry units collapsed in panic under the relentless tank onslaught.

There were no U.S. tanks in Korea, and the tanks in nearby Japan were light M-24 Chafee scout tanks. They were dispatched to Korea but could do little

The M60 series is in many ways representative of American tank design of the postwar years. It is not a particularly bold or imaginative design, but enjoys the good reliability of a well-proven design. Michael Green

good with their peewee 75mm tank gun. The tide was not turned until the U.S. Army managed to scrape together some real tank units, equipped with the wartime-vintage M-4 Sherman and the M-26 Pershing heavy tank.

The Sherman and the T-34-85 were contemporaries, and a pretty even match. The M-26 Pershing heavy tank, too late to have seen much combat in Europe in 1945, was finally tested in battle. It was a good design, and was the ancestor of all American medium tanks up to today's M1 Abrams tank. It was more than a match for the smaller T-34-85. Its real Soviet counterpart, the IS-3 Stalin heavy tank, was not provided to the Koreans. If these two had met, it would have been a tough fight.

The North Korean tanks were formidable when facing badly armed infantry in the first weeks of the fighting. Facing real opposition, they were soundly trounced. It wasn't so much the technological balance that decided the contest. There wasn't that much difference in firepower, armor, and mobility between both sides. Crew training and experience were far more critical. The American and other UN forces had a decided advantage in that respect. The final score in the tank fighting was five North Korean tanks knocked out for every U.S. tank destroyed. Tank fighting petered out in late 1950 after nearly all the North Korean armor had been destroyed. More than half the North Korean tanks were destroyed by air attack. The UN forces continued to use tanks for infantry support until the cease-fire was announced in 1953.

The Korean fighting highlighted the deficiencies of the U.S. tank force. The T-34-85 was not the best Soviet tank. It was being replaced in Soviet units by the T-54A, an excellent new design with a very potent 100mm gun. With the cold war heating up, new attention was paid to rearming the American tank force. The M-26 was joined in Korea by the M-46, a modernized derivative with automotive improvements. It was followed by the M-47 Patton tank, which became operational too late for combat in Korea. The M-47 introduced a sophisticated fire control system to permit greater accuracy at longer ranges.

The turret layout was clumsy, and most M-47s were unloaded on overseas allies.

The most successful of the U.S. tanks of the 1950s was the M-48 Patton. The M-48 introduced a turret patterned after the Soviet-style cast hemispherical designs. Although its armament was essentially the same as that of the M-26 of 1944, it had a variety of novel features. Its ballistic shape was a considerable improvement over the Pershing family, giving it greater protection for the weight. It had only four crewmen. The fifth crewman on tanks until the M-48 was a codriver/machine gunner, and his tasks were not essential.

The early models of the M-48 were plagued with technical difficulties brought about by the haste with which the tank was rushed into production. In some respects, it was a conservative design. Its gun was barely adequate to deal with contemporary Soviet tanks, such as the T-55. The M-48 was still powered by a gasoline engine, long after most armies had switched over to diesels. Gasoline engines are a real hazard in combat due to the risk of fire if the engine area is hit. In contrast, diesel fuel is very difficult to ignite.

Many of these problems were corrected with later models of the Patton, such as the M48A3. This model finally introduced a diesel engine. The M-48 remained the mainstay of the U.S. Army into the 1960s and saw combat with both army and marine tank units in Vietnam. Widely exported, it was used with considerable success by the Israeli army in the 1967 Mideast war and also saw action with Pakistani tank units in the 1965 war over Kashmir. Quite remarkably, it is still in service in several NATO armies. A modernized M-48, the M48A5, is still in service with the U.S. Army's National Guard tank battalions. And the German army, the Bundeswehr, still uses a locally modified version, the M48A2G2, in its reserve formations.

During the Hungarian uprising in Budapest in 1956, insurgent Hungarian troops drove a spanking new Soviet T-54A tank into the British Embassy compound. This was the first clear glimpse that western intelligence had of this tank, even though the Soviets had it in production for nearly a decade. It was a shock. Although it was ten tons lighter than the M-48 Patton, it was better armored. Indeed, there was real question whether the 90mm gun on the M-48 could penetrate its frontal armor. The U.S. Army tankers had the uneasy feeling that they were back to the same sorry situation faced by their 1944 counterparts against the German Panther. The solution to this dilemma was to improve the ammunition for the 90mm gun and to look for a new gun. It proved to be a British-designed 105mm. The U.S. Army was considering the adoption of a radically new tank, the T-95, to replace the M-48. It opted instead for a major modernization of the M-48 design with the new 105mm gun added. The resulting tank was the M-60, which for thirty years has been the mainstay of the U.S. Army's tank battalions.

The rugged M-60 is in many respects typical of American tank design since World War II. Because it is a modest elaboration of the proven M-48 design, it is extremely reliable. This is no small thing in a tank and should not be underestimated. Tanks are mechanically complex machines that operate in the most appalling of conditions. They are expected to perform equally well in the sweltering rot of a dank tropical jungle and in the subarctic cold of northern Norway. Many tanks have desirable combat features

The M60A1 was the backbone of the U.S. Army tank forces from the time of the Vietnam war up to the early 1980s. In the wake of the 1973 Mideast war, it was apparent to tankers that it was too poorly protected to survive in modern tank combat. A new design with better armor was the objective of the new XM-1 program. U.S. Army/DoD

on paper yet fail in this key ingredient. A sizzling hot tank design with a powerful gun and effective armor is just a big, useless hunk of rusting metal if it can't be kept moving. The German Panther tank is a good example. It was a killer tank, much better armed than its puny Allied opponents such as the American Sherman and the dreadful British Cromwell. But it was especially mechanically complex and suffered a far higher breakdown rate than the dependable Sherman.

The M-60's British counterpart, the Chieftain, is another sorry example of this typical tank disease. The Chieftain promised to be an absolutely crushing machine. Its armor is much thicker than that of the M-60 (to an extent that is still classified). Its sleek, elegant turret shape is superior in ballistic design to the slabby mediocrity of the M-60 turret. The Chieftain is armed with an awesome 120mm gun. But the Chieftain had a cranky new engine that left the tank immobile all too often. It was long derided as NATO's ''best pillbox'' until the engine problems were gradually solved in the 1970s.

But the M-60 had its vices as well. It was needlessly large and heavy; its German counterpart, the Leopard 1, was armed with the same 105mm gun but was much more compact and twelve tons lighter, due to less armor. Like many tanks designed under peacetime conditions, the M-60 had some features ill suited to the realities of tank combat. This would become very evident in the Mideast war of 1973.

The wars between Israel and its Arab neighbors have proven to be the seminal events in postwar tank design. The 1973 war was particularly influential. These battles pitted many of the best NATO tank designs against the best Soviet designs. The tank battles were fought on a scale unmatched since the great tank duels of World War II. And they involved new antitank technologies, such as the guided antitank missile. In 1973, the Israeli army was equipped with American M-48 and M-60 and British Centurion tanks. The M-60s were used largely as manufactured with very modest local changes. The British Centurions had been heavily rebuilt, with the Israeli Ordnance Corps replacing their engine and power train

with the type found in the more dependable M-60 series. The M-60 series was most heavily used on the Sinai front against Egypt, whereas the Centurion was extensively used in the Golan Heights against Syria.

The fighting highlighted many problems with the M-60, which is fitted with a hydraulic turret traverse system. Such systems have been used since the M-4 Sherman in World War II. The main attraction of hydraulic traverse compared to electric traverse is that it allows much faster turret travel. This is a very important advantage in close-range tank duels, as American tankers found in Europe in 1944–45 and in Korea in 1950. The problem with such a system is that the hydraulic fluid is under considerable pressure. If the fluid lines are ruptured when the tank is hit, they spray the inside of the turret with a flammable mist. During the 1973 war, this happened on a number of occasions, burning tank crews badly. To make matters worse, the M-60 stores much of its ammunition in the rear turret bustle. Turrets tend to take a disproportionate share of the hits during combat. When the ammunition is hit, the flammable propellant is easily ignited. Once one round is ignited, it tends to set off neighboring rounds in rapid succession. The turret becomes a searing blast furnace in a matter of seconds.

The high crew casualties in the M-60 tank units proved to be demoralizing to the Israelis. Tankers with a choice selected duty in the Centurion battalions. The Centurion uses electric turret traverse, reducing the fire hazard, and most of the ammunition was located lower in the hull. The Israelis began to solve the problem on the M-60s with local modifications and American help. The hydraulic fluid problem, not fully appreciated until the 1973 war, could be dealt with by adopting a less flammable fluid and Halon fire suppressing systems. The Israelis also began moving much of the tank's ammunition into the lower hull, as had been done with the Centurion. The M-60 had proven to be a reliable and adequate fighting machine. But shortcomings in its performance raised serious questions about its capabilities against future Soviet tanks. The fighting convinced both the Israeli and American armies that a new tank design was needed.

All along, the U.S. Army had considered the M-60 an interim solution. All hopes had been placed on a new joint German-American tank, the MBT-70 main battle tank. It had been under study since 1963, only a few years after M-60 deployment had begun.

The MBT-70 program was a quest for the perfect tank. It was undoubtedly the most complicated and sophisticated tank design ever seriously considered by any major army, even compared to tanks today. There is the old adage, popular with engineers, that perfection is the enemy of excellence. Engineering is by its very nature a matter of compromise. The

The U.S. Army did try out some revolutionary ideas in tank designs in the 1960s and 1970s. But they were just too revolutionary, like the MBT–70 tank. The failure of the MBT–70 program, and earlier *overambitious efforts like the T–95, left the army no choice but to continue to manufacture uninspired designs like the M-60 much past their prime. U.S. Army/DoD*

28

best possible design is never perfect. The merely excellent is judged unacceptable and the futile quest for the ideal blunders on.

The program was saddled by the politically inspired deadweight of American-German cooperation. It was the hope that such a program would reduce the inefficient redundancy of each major NATO army having its own tank. Unfortunately, the cooperative effort proved far too difficult in practice. American designers used English measurement (inches and feet), whereas the Germans used metric. Typically, the American team was not conversant in German, and German documentation had to be laboriously and expensively translated into English. (Many of the Germans were bilingual.) These difficulties caused unanticipated delays and cost overruns. Beyond these problems, the tank was inordinately complex.

In place of a conventional gun system, the MBT-70 was designed around a new type of gun that could fire either guided antitank missiles or conventional projectiles. The gun fire control system was stabilized to allow the tank to fire on the move. The driver was located in the turret with the rest of the crew, to permit the use of a fully enclosed compartment protected against chemical and nuclear contamination. The hydropneumatic suspension allowed the tank to crouch down to lower its profile to the enemy. All this complexity came at a high price. The army could ill afford such a tank with its budget being drained by the Vietnam War. The German Bundeswehr withdrew its support in 1969 due to the cost problem. The U.S. Army decided to go it alone, renaming a more austere version of the MBT-70 as the XM-803. It clung to life until 1971, when it was finally cancelled. In light of the lessons of the 1973 war, its demise proved fortuitous in the long run.

One of the only aspects of the MBT-70 program to show up as real hardware in the hands of U.S. Army troops was the ill-fated 152mm Shillelagh gun system. The principal antitank projectile for this weapon was the unique Shillelagh missile, which promised great accuracy at long ranges, even if it cost nearly thirty times as much as a conventional antitank projectile. The new gun system was also technologically attractive, since it could be mounted on both light tanks and main battle tanks, such as the M-60. The army had been developing a new scout tank along with the MBT-70, the M-551 Sheridan, and this entered service in 1968. The Sheridan was armed with the Shillelagh gun/missile system. The army also decided to arm some of the M-60s with this revolutionary new weapon. This version was called the M60A2.

The Shillelagh system was a disappointment to say the least. The M-551 Sheridan tanks were rushed prematurely into combat in Vietnam. The gun system was not fully proven and the combat environment was not suitable for demonstrating its heavy antitank firepower. North Vietnamese tank attacks were uncommon at this stage of the war. The Sheridan had terrible teething problems, which persisted even when the vehicle was issued to armored cavalry units in Germany in the early 1970s. The gun/missile system was just too much for a light tank. When firing the conventional projectile, the tank was so badly jarred that the gun fire control system could be knocked out of alignment. There were a series of accidental turret fires caused by the projectile casing rupturing. After only a decade in service, a short time for an American tank, the Sheridan was retired in 1979. The only unit retaining them is the tank battalion of the 82d Airborne Division. The airborne forces need a light tank capable of being easily airlifted, and the Sheridan is the only tank capable of filling the bill. The Sheridan soldiers on in small numbers and saw combat again in 1989 during the fighting in Panama as part of Operation Just Cause.

The main problem with the Sheridan is its overly ambitious weapon system, not the tank itself. Its basic chassis, like most American tank designs of the 1960s, is durable and reliable. The army had more than a thousand Sheridans in mothballs in the 1980s, and so decided to use them in the training role at the National Training Center. It is in this role that we will again meet the Sheridan later in this book.

The Sheridan mess was repeated with the M60A2. The program suffered serious cost overruns and was the subject of unusually critical congressional attention. In service, the M60A2 was dubbed the "Starship," an unaffectionate reference to the complexities of its gun fire controls. Congress was so soured by this string of fiascos—the MBT-70, the Sheridan, and the M60A2—that it was unusually skeptical of succeeding army tank programs.

By the mid-1970s, the U.S. Army's tank force was in sorry shape. The M-60A1 was an adequate design, but it was reaching the end of its evolutionary possibilities. It compared poorly in armor and firepower to other NATO designs such as the Chieftain and was arthritic compared to the German Leopard I. But more importantly, it compared very badly to newly discovered Soviet tank types such as the T-64 and T-72. However, improvements were made to the M-60, which resulted in the M60A3. It had more effective armor, a much superior fire control system, and better automotive performance than the M-60A1. But its evolutionary potential had nearly ended.

A TANKER'S TANK

Preoccupied with the Vietnam War and all the troubles that ensued in the years after the war, the U.S. Army had paid too little attention to its main mission on NATO's central front. The Soviets relentlessly pushed ahead with their tank efforts, unimpeded by the problems besetting the U.S. Army, whose development community failed to appreciate the pace of Soviet tank developments. In 1967, the Soviets fielded the T-64 tank. Although fifteen tons lighter than the M-60A1, it was armed with a 125mm smoothbore gun, easily outperforming the 105mm gun on the M-60A1. And it incorporated advanced ceramic armor inserts, the first use of nonmetallic armor on a tank. The U.S. Army didn't get its first clear hints about the T-64 until 1970, and by 1972 another new Soviet tank appeared, the T-72. It too was superior to the M-60A1 in most respects. The army's sad lack of foresight prolonged an unfortunate tradition of underestimating the capabilities of foreign tank designers.

The confluence of events, the lessons of the 1973 war and the appearance of the new Soviet tanks, helped to shake the army out of its post–Vietnam War lethargy. The army began designing a new tank, which would emerge in the late 1970s as the M1 Abrams. It would prove to be a rarity in American tank history, a tank clearly superior to its most likely opposition, a tank inspired by combat-experienced tankers, not computer analysts.

Chapter 2

Abrams

The lessons of the 1973 Mideast war forced the U.S. Army to refocus its attention on the essential requirements of tank combat. The MBT-70 design was burdened by too much gimmickry that did not add substantially to the tank's combat power in battle. The new tank would have to survive on an increasingly dangerous battlefield. But it would also have to be designed and manufactured within the constrained defense budgets of the post–Vietnam War years.

The new U.S. Army tank program received three lucky breaks. First, the 1973 war demonstrated that the tank remained the central element in modern ground combat and provided a wealth of important technical information. Second, many of the key army leaders connected with the program had been tankers in World War II and were intent to field a tank superior to the opposition. Third, the British army proved willing to share a key new breakthrough in tank armor, code-named Burlington.

The heavy tank losses on both sides in the 1973 war led the press in Europe and America to conclude that the tank was dead. Guided antitank missiles seemed to herald an end to armored vehicles much as the longbow had signaled the end of the armored knight on the battlefield of Crécy in 1346. The U.S. Army took a close look at the lessons of the war with the cooperation of the Israeli army. The guided antitank missile proved to be less central to the heavy tank losses than was first believed. Only a tenth of the tank losses were from missiles. The vast majority of losses on both sides were caused by tank guns.

However, the widespread use of the RPG-7 antitank grenade launcher was worrisome. Unlike the guided antitank missiles, which were expensive and so deployed in small numbers, the RPG-7 was everywhere. Weapons such as these had been around since World

Contemporary tank designs were heavily influenced by the lessons of the 1973 Mideast war. Here, the burned out hulks of an Egyptian T–55 and an Israeli M48A2 stand in grim reminder of the fury of the battles. Israeli Government Press Agency

War II, but recent advances in warhead technology had made them far more deadly. The small shaped-charge warhead on the RPG-7 could penetrate the armor of the M-60 tank and most other tanks of its generation. Even smaller antitank rockets, such as the U.S. Army's M72 LAW (light antitank weapon), were bound to show up in the Warsaw Pact countries eventually. Soon, every infantryman would have a weapon capable of defeating a half-million-dollar main battle tank. Something had to be done about the shaped-charge menace.

Privately, the U.S. Army was critical of Israeli tank tactics. Although the Israeli army was highly respected for its proven combat skills, it was not flawless. Israeli battle groups were tank heavy. They were not adequately supported by infantry or artillery.

The U.S. Army's search for a new tank in the 1970s led to a competition between two tank designs, one by General Motors, one by Chrysler. Here, the proto-type of the Chrysler XM-1, which would emerge several years later as the winner of the M1 Abrams development program. U.S. Army/DoD

Many U.S. tankers felt that the Israelis could have avoided the problems with the Egyptian antitank missile teams by paying more attention to NATO-style combined arms tactics. Guided missile teams are vulnerable to preventive artillery fire. Accompanying infantry can flush out and eliminate hidden antitank squads.

The 1973 war provided a wealth of other technical lessons. Although the Syrians and Egyptians did not have the most modern Soviet equipment, their combat operations were close enough to give an accurate picture of how the Soviet army would fight and how well its weapons were likely to perform. The war underlined the shortcomings in American tanks; for example, the problems with tank fires and the need for improved night-fighting equipment. But the war also underlined important vulnerabilities in Soviet equipment and tactics. It suggested that a small force, with well-trained tankers, could conduct a successful defense against a much larger force composed of tankers with mediocre training and leadership. These lessons had a clear bearing on the nature of the NATO–Warsaw Pact balance.

The task force set up in 1972 to develop the new tank was headed by Gen. William Desobry, commander of the Armor Center at Fort Knox. Desobry had been tank commander during the Battle of the Bulge in 1944. He could count on support from another World War II tanker, Gen. Creighton Abrams. In 1972, Abrams was still commander of U.S. forces in Vietnam. But with U.S. involvement in the war winding down, he was appointed chief of staff of the U.S. Army. Abrams was a dyed-in-the-wool tanker who recalled his experiences in World War II tank combat with considerable pride. Abrams provided important support to the new tank program, which soon became the army's highest priority weapons development effort. Army leaders such as Abrams and Desobry vividly remembered the unsettling feeling of sitting in an M-4 tank against a superior Panther. They had no intention of allowing this to be repeated in their sons' generation.

The third fortuitous event in the new program was a British discovery. In the late 1960s, Dr. Gilbert

The odd angular shape of the M1 Abrams stands in sharp contrast to the sleekly armored turrets of tanks of the 1960s. The reason was the invention of radically new Burlington armor. U.S. Army/DoD

33

Harvey, a researcher at the Royal Ordnance Research and Development Establishment in Chobham, England, made a critical breakthrough in armor technology. Until the 1970s, tank armor had been based on various steel alloys. There had been some experimentation with steel and ceramic laminates, but these didn't appear to be cost-effective. While investigating ways to protect fuel cells, Harvey discovered that certain honeycomb structures tended to diminish the effects of shaped charges. Further research led to a novel armor configuration, code-named Burlington. It is more commonly known as Chobham armor, after the location of its development. The British army decided to share its secret with its American allies. Tankers such as Abrams and Desobry were startled by the remarkable performance of Burlington armor during its demonstrations in the United States. Burlington armor promised a major leap forward in tank protection, especially against the menace of the shaped charge.

Symbolic of the fresh start that the new tank represented, it was dubbed XM-1. The Department of Defense had become enamored of competitive development programs as a way to ensure the lowest cost and the best possible product. As a result, two separate tanks were designed to meet the XM-1 requirement, one by Chrysler and one by General Motors (GM). Both designs incorporated an improved version of Chobham armor developed by the Ballistics Research Lab (BRL) at Aberdeen Proving Grounds, Maryland. In less than four years, the two firms were able to turn over prototype tanks to the U.S. Army. Tests would be conducted to see which tank best matched army tactical requirements and the army budget.

The tests were inconclusive. Both designs were highly satisfactory, with the General Motors tank hav-

An enduring controversy over the M1 Abrams has been its fuel consumption. The novel turbine engine selected by the Army consumes more fuel than a conventional diesel, but also offers better accelera- *tion and fewer maintenance headaches. Here, M1s are refueled by an old "Goer." These were replaced in the 1980s by the superior new generation HEMTT trucks.* Steven Zaloga

ing some advantages in armor layout and the Chrysler machine having advantages in automotive performance. The GM design was favored by many in the army, whereas other Department of Defense officials favored the more radical turbine-engined Chrysler design. All parties agreed it was a close fight.

The program was served a monkey wrench in the middle of deliberations. The Bundeswehr was also working on its own new tank, the Leopard II. At the time, NATO was contemplating a major buy of E-3A Sentry AWACS (airborne warning and command system) surveillance aircraft, with Germany paying a big portion of the bill. Many German officials strongly hinted that it would be only fair to have the U.S. Army consider the Leopard II along with the Chrysler and GM prototypes for the XM-1 require-

ment. A Leopard II prototype was tested, but it stood little chance of beating out either American design. The failed MBT-70 program had left a sour taste in the mouths of many army officials, and it was doubtful that influential congressmen would consent to accepting a German tank not built in their district. The German case was not helped by the unfinished nature of the prototype shipped to the United States. In the end, the U.S. did agree to consider adopting the Leopard II's 120mm gun on the XM-1. Chrysler and GM were sent back to the drawing boards to make certain that their designs could accommodate the German gun if necessary.

When the firms returned with new bids in 1976, the army concluded that Chrysler had proposed a more satisfactory package. The decision to go with the

Flying tank! No better example of the tremendous acceleration possible with the M1 Abrams 1500-hp engine. The desire for more speed in tanks was due to changes in Army doctrine which placed greater stress on maintaining the momentum of attack against enemy forces—a point validated in Desert Storm. Steven Zaloga

Chrysler presentation has been controversial to this day, but program officials had to choose between two very close designs.

Army officials had originally planned to name the new tank after Gen. George C. Marshall, but following the death of Creighton Abrams in 1974, the decision was changed. It was a particularly appropriate choice due to Abrams's long and distinguished connections with the U.S. Army's tank force, and his important role in moving the XM-1 program through the bureaucratic quagmires in Washington, D.C.

With the decision to go with the Chrysler version of the XM-1, development of the actual eleven production prototypes began. The test program proved to be controversial. To keep the unit cost for the tank to a bare minimum, in order to placate a cost-conscious Congress, the test program was compressed. Normally, tanks undergo developmental testing, which irons out technical problems in the design, and then operational testing, which examines the interface between the soldier and the machine. These were run concurrently, which exaggerated problems.

The XM-1 Abrams came under considerable congressional fire and eventually an onslaught of press criticism. Given the army's previous track record with the MBT-70 and the Sheridan, congressional concern was to be expected. But much of the press criticism was uninformed, at times bordering on the ludicrous. Sadly, a program that resulted in a first-rate tank, with a lower sticker price than comparable foreign designs, was depicted in the press as an overpriced lemon. In actuality, the army had finally come up with an excellent tank design. It was not a perfect tank, but perfect tanks, such as the overambitious MBT-70, usually end up in museums instead of in the hands of the troops.

Many critics, ignorant of tank development trends elsewhere in the world, were under the delusion that the Abrams's test problems were somehow unique to the M1 tank and atypical of tank development efforts in general. In fact, many of history's finest weapons had troubled development programs. This has been especially true of radically new weapons' designs, and the M1 was certainly radical. The T-34, which set the standard for tank designs in World War II, was almost completely ineffective when introduced into service in 1941. Its transmission led to frequent breakdowns, and Soviet industry had failed to provide sufficient reserves of ammunition and spare parts. But the T-34 proved to be a vital element in the Soviet victory in World War II. The M-48 Patton tanks spent most of the first few years after initial production mothballed in army warehouses owing to serious mechanical problems. Yet once these were corrected, the M-48 went on to be one of the most reliable tanks in U.S. Army history. Early models of the P-51 Mustang fighter, the best propeller fighter in the European theater of war in World War II, suffered from engine problems. The M1's start-up problems were not nearly as severe as these examples.

American tankers first got a feel for the advantages offered by the M1 in the autumn of 1982, when the Abrams was employed during the Carbine Fortress war games as part of the annual NATO Reforger exercises. A close look at this operation will help explain the M1's advances, and the continued primacy of the tank in maneuver warfare.

CARBINE FORTRESS

The countryside around Wurzburg is much like that of the rest of Bavaria. The rolling hills of the Main River valley are dotted with sleepy small towns. In the bright September sunshine, the orange roofs and white stucco walls that characterize the local German architecture provide a colorful contrast with the fluorescent lime green of the neighboring farmlands. As in most of Central Europe, the forests have given way to agriculture, but there are still the occasional woods of birch and spruce. Autumn in central Germany is a festive time. With the harvest collected, it's the season for the traditional Oktoberfest. The towns are soon awash in good beer and hearty sausages. As in much of Europe, the picturesque villages continue to suffer the intrusions of modern life. Gasoline stations and car dealerships mar the view of medieval town walls and the ruins of old castles. The stillness of Bavarian villages is rudely shaken by the passage of large trucks rumbling through the market squares with their loads of goods for the industrial cities farther north.

Autumn is the time for intrusions of another sort, the rumble of tank engines. Opel and BMW sedans are muscled out of the way by columns of tanks and tracked vehicles. The largest of the NATO war games, Reforger, is usually held in the autumn or early winter. With the harvest already in, the tanks and armored vehicles can exercise in the farm fields without causing expensive crop damage. Of the recent Reforger exercises, the 1982 war games were the most intriguing. Code-named Carbine Fortress, they marked the introduction of a new generation of tanks to Europe, the U.S. Army's M1 Abrams main battle tank. The revolutionary new features of the M1 Abrams permitted a new variety of fast-paced tactics and other innovations.

Operation Overload Hide pitted the 3d Battalion of the 64th Armored Regiment (3-64 Armor) with its new M1 tanks against a Canadian mechanized formation. The 3-64 Armor was a part of the fictitious Blue Army, defending against an invasion by the Orange Army. The commander of the 3-64 Armor, Lt. Col. John Kelsey, decided to attempt a novel tactic to deal with the opposing Orange forces. Rather than attack the invading Orange forces directly, he positioned his fifty Abrams tanks in a wooded area outside of the town of Dingolhausen, the objective of the enemy forces. The battalion was totally concealed but could defend itself if discovered. The aim was to allow the enemy formations to pass the hidden battalion, which would then counterattack the enemy's vulnerable rear area.

On the evening of 12 September, Kelsey's tanks moved into the wooded area in anticipation of the next day's attack. Once the tanks were in place, all engines were shut down and all headlights were turned off. The tankers were told to keep things quiet and to stay off the radio for fear of disclosing their position. The battalion remained undercover, in the enemy rear, for sixteen hours. Few of the crews got any sleep that night. The enemy invasion was expected to begin

first thing the next day. By early morning, there were sounds of enemy tracked vehicles moving across the farm fields and nearby woods. But the hidden battalion remained undiscovered.

John Kelsey described the scene: "They attacked on the open ground, the easiest routes around our hide position. We could physically see and hear the enemy vehicles going by us. When we were ordered to attack, we launched out and swept northeast, then south. We caught the enemy from behind. It was really a tanker's battle."

At 1200 Zulu time on 13 September, the 3-64 Armor had its first contact with Canadian infantry of the Orange Army. It was time to launch the counterattack. The drivers started up the tank engines and the tank crews prepared to move out. The M1's turbine

The M1 design placed greater stress on controlling vehicle visibility—hiding yourself as well as seeing the enemy first. For the first time in many years the tank had its own smoke generation system and smoke launchers. Less obviously, the M1 was the first tank fitted from the beginning with a thermal imaging sight, a critical ingredient in the Desert Storm tank battles. Greg Stewart

engine is far less noisy than the diesel engines used in most other tanks, such as the older M-60.

A driver with B Company recalled the opening moments of the attack: "When we cranked [the engines] you couldn't hear the tank running, even in the woods. I know they would have heard the engines of the M-60s. Once we started out of the woods, we ran into Canadian APCs, TOWs, and tanks."

The battle developed very quickly, beginning at five minutes past noon. One M1 Abrams company attacked the Canadian infantry company from behind, wiping out its M113 armored troop carriers without loss. The second company struck the right flank of a Canadian Leopard tank company that was already engaged in combat with friendly Blue forces of the 2-30 Infantry at Dingolhausen. This company was completely surprised and knocked out of the war. One of the Canadian officers with the enemy Orange Army later recalled: "One minute, it's quiet with no contact. The next minute you are overwhelmed—swarmed with quick, whispering death." Although the attack had not involved real ammunition, the effect of close-quarter tank attack on infantry was hard to forget. Another Canadian commander noted: "One of my soldiers awakened the following night, screaming over the experience."

The greatest success of Operation Overload Hide came on the far side of the attack. The third company of 3-64 Armor made a fast hook against the rear of the Canadian task force on the edge of the Steigerwald forest. The American tankers were surprised to find nine Canadian Leopard tanks lined up in a neat row being refueled. They were sitting ducks, and soon their orange maneuver beacons were flashing to signal their mock destruction. The pace of the action was ferocious.

An M1 Abrams tank commander, S. Sgt. Wesley Means, recalled: "Most of us were awake all night. But when we launched—Wow! The battle went quick. We killed a lot of Canadian infantry . . . massacred them. My platoon killed six Leopards . . . we only had four tanks."

Having dealt with the refueling Leopards, the M1 tank company then swung down onto the rear of an-other Canadian Leopard company. A friendly Blue Army attack helicopter unit with AH-1S Cobras popped up unexpectedly on the Canadian left flank, adding to the tank slaughter. After barely fifteen minutes of fighting, the Canadian task force had been wiped out.

The pace of the battle had been dictated by the new M1 Abrams and its ability to move and fight at high cross-country speeds. Previous generations of tanks had top road speeds of twenty-five to thirty miles per hour, but their cross-country speed was seldom better than fifteen miles per hour if the terrain was at all rough. The M1 Abrams can go from zero to twenty miles per hour in seven seconds—not impressive for an automobile but extremely impressive for a tank. Other tank commanders from the 64th Armored were quite surprised and pleased by the advantages offered by the M1's superior mobility.

On 15 September, a cavalry task force of the Orange Army began attacks on Blue Army tank units south of Giebelstadt. The Blue Army commander ordered the 2-64 Armor, located on the outer edge of the battle area, to make a sweeping run around Giebelstadt to strike the task force in the rear. The attack was launched at 1430 Zulu time. At 1500, helicopter scouts located the main Orange force, and the mass of 2-64 Armor swung south to attack them in the rear. In forty-five minutes of fighting, the Orange cavalry task force was wiped out, including two armored cavalry squadrons with tanks and armored personnel carriers.

Sergeant First Class Jeffrey Fields, a platoon leader with 2-64 Armor, remembers the encounter:
As we swung and faced the enemy you could see the mass confusion they were in with tracks and tanks nearly bumping into each other trying to get out of there. They were totally caught by surprise. What we had done was to do a complete 360-degree circle from where we had been at the start of the mission. We were moving so fast that you could see all the confusion it was causing the other side. It's just remarkable that you could have four tanks running in a pattern with the gun tubes oriented in the right direction and moving at 40 miles per hour.

The speed of the attacking unit made its assault seem almost irresistible. An M1 loader, Pfc. Curtis Sneckenberger, remarked: ''It seemed that the enemy didn't have a chance, even though they had us outnumbered.'' Throughout the exercise, Orange Army units had a hard time adjusting to the faster pace of operations made possible by the new tanks.

During the battle near Volkach, A Company of 1-64 Armor experimented with another little touch to sow confusion. At the outset of the attack, the M1 Abrams tanks turned on their smoke generators, obscuring the area completely. They were able to continue the attack, since their own tank sensors could see through the smoke. A tank commander remembered the incident: ''All those tanks lined up behind us, and we hit that smoke generator and hid 'em. We just hauled ass cross country. They just didn't know what hit 'em. We pushed 'em all the way back to Schweinfurt. Those M60s are dinosaurs.''

Innovative tactics and new equipment proved to be a powerful combination in the Carbine Fortress exercises. Commanders who expected the exercises

Tanks are only so much scrap metal without well trained crews. The advent of the M1 Abrams was marked also by major improvements in tank training simulators as well as expanded tanker training programs such as here at the National Training Center. This combination of revolutionary technology and radically improved training resulted in the lopsided victory in Desert Storm. Greg Stewart

to fall into the same predictable pattern as in the past soon found their units swamped and overwhelmed by the highly mobile M1 Abrams tank platoons of the 64th Armored. The commander of 1-64 Armor recalls the fighting near Schweinfurt on 21 September: *The second day was the most devastating. We had two of my M1 companies and 3-64 Armor attacking on line in the Bowling Alley West. That was a magnificent sight. We really completely overwhelmed the Orange forces. There was nothing they could have thrown up there to keep our two battalions from rolling right on through. . . . They absolutely could not react to the speed of that tank, no matter how hard they tried. And they tried harder and harder every day to plug their holes. But once we found the hole, we were through it and in their rear so fast, they just could not react. We kept them disrupted, confused, and just generally frustrated for three days.*

The debut of the M1 Abrams tank at Carbine Fortress highlights the value of the tank in modern warfare. It is not simply the armor, impressive as it is. It is not simply the firepower, as deadly as it is. It is not simply the mobility, as fast as it is. It is the combination of these features—armor, firepower, and

An M1 Abrams on gunnery exercise at Fort Hood, Texas. The gun of the M1, a 105mm rifled type, was no different than that on the M60A1. But the fire- control system offered important improvements in accuracy. Michael Green

mobility—that makes tank units the shock troops in modern land warfare. But the Carbine Fortress exercise highlighted another key lesson. Equipment alone does not win wars. No matter how improved a new tank may be over older tanks, it will have little impact in the hands of unskilled troops. It was the imaginative use of the new M1 Abrams tank that gave it such a big impact during the 1982 war games.

THE ABRAMS IN DESERT STORM

The M1 Abrams real test came in 1991 During Operation Desert Storm. The first armor units deployed to the Gulf in August 1990 included the 82nd Airborne Division's M551 Sheridan armor battalion, and M60A1 tanks of the U.S. Marine Corps carried on maritime pre-positioning ships located at Diego Garcia in peacetime. The first M1 battalions to mobilize were those of the 24th Infantry Division (Mechanized), headquartered during peacetime at Fort Stewart in Georgia. The 24th Infantry's tank battalions were deployed by ship, arriving in the autumn of 1990. They were still mostly equipped with the initial M1 or IPM1 versions of the Abrams, but it was later decided to move in the improved M1A1 Abrams from pre-positioned stores in Europe. By the time of the 1991 ground offensive, the majority of U.S. tanks in the Gulf were the M1A1 version of the Abrams. The 24th Mechanized Infantry Division served as the heavy shock force of the U.S. Army's 18th Airborne Corps; the other major units included the 82nd Airborne and the 101st Airmobile Divisions.

The decision in November 1990 to prepare the multi-national coalition forces for offensive land operations to liberate Kuwait meant that additional maneuver divisions would be needed. This came in the form of the U.S. Army's 7th Corps, stationed in Germany. During the winter of 1990–1991, heavy divisions including the 1st Armored, 1st Cavalry, 1st Infantry, and 3rd Armored Divisions were moved to Saudi Arabia. Other heavy formations included both the 2nd and 3rd Armored Cavalry Regiments. All these maneuver forces were equipped with the M1 or M1A1 tank in their tank battalions.

The U.S. Marine Corps deployed five tank battalions to the Gulf, including one on board ships off the Kuwaiti coast. Four were equipped with the M60A1 tank, and one (with the 2nd Division) was reequipped with the M1A1 tank from Army stockpiles. The Marines were supported by an Army armor brigade from the 2nd Armored Division, codenamed Tiger Brigade during Operation Desert Storm.

The operational plan for the ground offensive was shaped by the capabilities of the United States and coalition forces. The most mobile forces were those of the U.S. Army. A U.S. Army heavy division (tank or mechanized infantry) has ten to eleven line battalions of tanks or mechanized infantry on Bradley IFVs. In addition, all of its artillery is self-propelled. In contrast, a U.S. Marine division has only a single tank battalion, one mechanized battalion using AAV-7A1 amtracs, and a mechanized battalion using LAV light armored vehicles. As a result, the Army was given the task of making the sweeping end run to the west of the Kuwaiti border, while the Marine Corps divisions were committed to a direct frontal attack into Kuwait, aiming at Kuwait City.

Allied forces in the campaign were considerable. The Arab forces, including Saudi, Egyptian, Syrian and other Gulf state units, were mainly committed along the Kuwaiti coast and into Kuwait to the west of the U.S. Marine divisions. The French armored forces, including a single tank unit (the 4th Dragoon Regiment with AMX-30B2 tanks) was committed to the west of the U.S. Army's 18th Airborne Corps as a screening force to protect the entire left flank of the Allied drive. The British 1st Armoured Division, similar in capability to a U.S. Army heavy division, fought alongside the U.S. Army heavy divisions, pushing up along the Iraq-Kuwait border along the Wadi-al-Batin.

The attack on 24 February quickly achieved all of its objectives. Tank battles broke out almost immediately. The engagements were almost entirely one-sided. The Iraqi crews were very poorly trained compared to their adversaries and few proved capable of hitting the advancing Allied tanks. U.S. Army tank units were able to take advantage of the superior fire controls of the M1A1 Abrams and destroy Iraqi tanks before the Iraqis could effectively engage them. A very large fraction of the Iraqi tank force had already been destroyed from the air, especially in the forward areas. Most of the forward Iraqi units were infantry divisions with only a single battalion of twenty-five to thirty-five tanks. These were quickly overwhelmed. The first large-scale tank battles began when the British 1st Armoured Division swung towards Kuwait and began engaging the Iraqi 12th Armored Division. The British Challengers destroyed over forty Iraqi tanks in two days of fighting with no loss to themselves.

By 25 February, 270 Iraqi tanks had been destroyed in the ground fighting and Allied losses were remarkably light. The pace of the tank fighting picked up considerably on 26 February, as the Allied units began running into the Republican Guards divisions along the northern Kuwaiti frontier.

The rapid pace of the 7th Corps' battle—made possible in no small measure to the new generation of mechanized equipment like the Abrams, Challenger, Bradley and Warrior—could not be matched by the Iraqis. The momentum of the attack caused

The new M1A1 version of the Abrams introduced a new gun, the 120mm smoothbore, and more effective armor. Even with the added armor, tankers instinctively seek out hull-down positions—terrain features which hide the bulk of the tank from enemy fire while still allowing their own tank a good field of fire. Michael Green

most Iraqi units to remain frozen in place, fighting from prepared positions. Iraqi tanks were systematically destroyed by attack helicopters in the vanguard of the assault, or by direct fire from Allied tank units. The M1A1 Abrams tanks of the 2nd Armored Cavalry Regiment crashed through the Republican Guard 3rd Tawakalna Mechanized Division. In an engagement south of Nasiriya, the 24th Infantry Division caught an Iraqi T-72 brigade that was being loaded on tank transporters and trying to escape. The Iraqis lost all fifty tanks in moments.

Several Republican Guards units did make determined actions to stop the advance. Elements of the Republican Guards 2nd Medina Armored Division, and later the 1st Hammurabi Division confronted tanks of the U.S. Army's 1st and 3rd armored divisions on 25–26 February, but were decimated. The 24th Infantry Division dealt with the remainder of the Hammurabi Division in similar fashion. The United States did lose a small number of Bradleys to tank fire, but no M1 Abrams or Challengers were destroyed by Iraqi tank fire. The M1A1's thermal sights proved very handy in the poor weather conditions, and contrary to the widespread press allegations about reliability problems, the Abrams had no difficulty in staying in operation during the course of the rapid advance. By 27 February, the Iraqis had lost 700 tanks in ground fighting. Allied tank losses were four, mainly to mines.

The heaviest tank fighting inside Kuwait itself took place around the Kuwait City International Airport between U.S. Marine tanks and dug-in Iraqi defenders of the 3rd Tank Division. The Iraqi resistance was overcome, and the M1A1 Abrams Tiger Brigade accompanying the Marines was able to leapfrog ahead, helping to cut the road between Kuwait City and Basra to the north. It was a scene straight out of hell as the Tiger Brigade shot up dozens of vehicles trying to flee, with aircraft contributing to the slaughter. The area became known as Death's Highway, seven miles of burnt-out, bombed and blasted tanks, armored vehicles and trucks. It was hauntingly reminiscent of the great killing ground in Normandy in the summer of 1944 when the allied forces trapped the German Army units trying to flee through the Falaise Gap.

The fighting gradually petered out after the multinational forces declared a truce. Some Iraqi units, not hearing of the truce, kept fighting. In one engagement, a company of M1A1 Abrams tanks of the 3rd Armored Division, outnumbered three-to-one, engaged and destroyed forty Iraqi tanks and armored vehicles without a single loss. A similar battle in the 24th Mechanized Infantry's sector was equally one-sided.

The 1991 Desert Storm operation clearly demonstrated the combat capabilities of the M1 Abrams. It was able to engage opposing tanks at the outer limits of its engagement envelope and secure hit after hit. Seven Abrams tanks were hit, mainly by 125mm fire from T-72s, but no crewmen were lost as a result of the hits. The controversial thermal sights proved to be highly effective in acquiring targets even under poor weather conditions. The high speed of the Abrams helped keep up the momentum of the attack. And press allegations of the poor reliability of the Abrams were not borne out by actual combat experience.

LEOPARD II

To put the Abrams tank program into perspective, it's worth taking a look at some of the Abrams's foreign counterparts. When the 1973 Mideast war sent shock waves throughout the world's armies, not only did the U.S. Army decide it needed a new tank, but so did the German, French, British, and Israeli armies. The French program got sidetracked and emerged only in the 1990s with the AMX Leclerc. But by the early 1980s, the German Leopard II, British Challenger, and Israeli Merkava were being put into service.

The German Leopard II tank is closest to the M1 Abrams in design philosophy and performance. This is not altogether surprising. Germany and the United States had been involved in the MBT-70 debacle, and although they each had their own point of view, they drew many similar conclusions. Although they share a common name, the Leopard I and the Leopard II have nothing in common. The Leopard I is a fairly conventional design, being lighter and more agile than its American contemporary, the M-60A1, but having an identical main gun. Its basic armor is not as thick as the M-60A1's.

The German Bundeswehr set many of the same priorities as the U.S. Army in designing its new tank, but there were some crucial differences. The U.S. Army decided that advances in tank ammunition would make the standard 105mm gun sufficiently lethal for the foreseeable future. The Germans felt that a larger caliber gun might be needed to deal with future advances in Soviet armor. Prototypes of the Leopard II were built with both the 105mm gun and a new 120mm gun developed by Rheinmetall. The Germans were not keen on the idea of a turbine engine, feeling that its high fuel consumption did not justify its other advantages, such as quieter performance and improved acceleration. But like the U.S. Army, the Bundeswehr wanted a big engine to give major improvements in cross-country speed. The Germans were convinced that their well-seasoned automotive industry could provide them with a diesel engine that was both compact and rugged. The challenge in de-

It was the 1982 Reforger exercise in Germany in 1982 that helped to clarify the advantage of the new generation of main battle tanks. The speed of the M1, thought by many to be a mere frill, was fright- *eningly effective against forces using older generations of tanks and armored vehicles.* U.S. Army/ DoD

The M1A1's natural environment is in the farm fields and forests of Germany, the terrain in which it *was expected to fight. Ironically, its combat debut came in the open deserts of Iraq.* Michael Green

signing a diesel engine in the 1,500-horsepower range is it must not only be powerful but also quite light and compact.

The German program began in the late 1960s due to the decision to withdraw from the troubled MBT-70 effort. The first prototypes of the Leopard II were ready for trials in 1973, ahead of the XM-1 Abrams. The Leopard II program was far more protracted than the Abrams program, for a variety of reasons. The Germans were not aware of Burlington armor, so the initial prototypes of the Leopard II used a more conventional armor layout. By early 1974, the Germans expressed interest in competing in the XM-1 program, offering the Leopard II as an alternative to the Chrysler and General Motors prototypes. Clearly, there was a need to incorporate Burlington armor into the design. The Germans realized that they had a problem on their hands due to the poor protection of the Leopard II compared to that of the American XM-1 prototypes. Details of German participation in the Burlington armor program remain hidden. As a result, the entire armor layout of the tank turret had to be redesigned. This considerably delayed the program. In the interim, the Bundeswehr decided to go with the new 120mm gun. But their hopes concerning American interest in the Leopard II ran aground over American concerns about its armor layout and the usual difficulties of selling a foreign tank design to a major tank-producing nation.

The Leopard II finally arrived on the scene in 1979, several months before the first M1 Abrams. The Leopard II has proven to be a highly successful design, though not without the normal amount of start-up problems. The new gun, for example, caused some headaches. Most armies do not subject their tanks to as extensive an array of tests as the U.S. Army, which prefers to place the tanks in the hands of troops as soon as possible and gradually iron out the bugs. In the case of the Leopard II, one of the main problems centered around its new gun ammunition.

Most tank gun ammunition is configured much the same as rifle ammunition; that is, there is a projectile attached to a brass case that contains the powder propellant. (One minor difference is that tank guns now use aluminum/steel cases rather than the conventional brass cases.) When the tank gun is fired, the metal casing is ejected into a bin behind the gun. These spent casings present a problem, because tank interiors are small and soon become impossibly full of shell cases. During combat, it's often not safe to open up a hatch and toss out the litter! For that reason, there has long been interest in consumable cases; these use a combustible material instead of metal for the casing, which burns up when the gun is fired. The Shillelagh gun system developed for the MBT-70 used this system, but there were considerable headaches with it, as mentioned above.

The Germans adopted a semiconsumable case instead. Most of the case is combustible, but the back end, called the stub casing, is metal. This makes the round more durable, and the small stub casing that is ejected into the tank interior after firing is not large enough to create space problems. The difficulties the Bundeswehr encountered with the ammunition weren't due to the ammunition itself but to unexpected interactions between the new track and the ammunition stowage racks. The Bundeswehr adopted a metal-faced track for the Leopard II, which offers longer life than rubber-faced tracks, such as those on the M1. This is no insignificant detail. Track is the most expensive item on tanks that has to be replaced due to wear and tear even during peacetime. A set of tracks costs about $50,000 and lasts only a few thousand kilometers. The problem is that metal-faced track, although economical, can cause vibration problems. Vibrations at high speeds are transmitted through the metal hull of the Leopard II to the ammunition and loosen the casings of the ammunition. This is a serious matter: If the propellant begins to spill out, it is a fire hazard, since it is as volatile as solid rocket propellant. Also, a loose case loaded into the breech can jam the gun. For a number of months, the Leopard IIs were restricted from high-speed travel when carrying ammunition while the problem was worked out. Eventually, isolating the ammunition racks with dampers solved the problem. It is seemingly minor problems such as this that highlight the complexity of modern tank designs.

The Leopard II has gone on to become one of NATO's premier main battle tanks. Indeed, the Germans argue with some pride that it is *the* premier NATO main battle tank. It has done very well in the biannual Canadian Army Trophy (CAT) meets, which are staged to illustrate tank gunnery standards. Units from most NATO armies stationed in Germany show up to demonstrate their prowess. In recent years, the competition has been dominated by two tanks: the M1 Abrams and the Leopard II. In the last meet, in 1989, Leopard II units took six of the top spots, followed by an M1A1 unit. (The M1 Abrams still holds the honors for the highest score ever achieved, at CAT '87.) Interestingly enough, the Dutch Leopard II units have been among the top performers at CAT. Dutch troops have the reputation in NATO as long-haired hippy freaks due to their lax dress regulations, but their tank crews have consistently scored in the top half-dozen tank platoons, and often number one. The Leopard II serves with the German, Dutch, and Swiss armies, and is being considered by the Swedish army.

CHALLENGER

Britain's path to a new main battle tank was somewhat more tortuous than in the case of Germany and the

The business end of the tank. The essence of tank fighting is the same as it was in 1918: find the enemy first and hit him before he hits you. Michael Green

The M1A1 Abrams was first deployed to Germany, leaving stateside units such as the 24th Infantry Division with the older M1. Before the outbreak of Desert Storm, many of the stateside units were re-equipped with the more potent new version.
Michael Green

United States. The Chieftain was much better armed and armored than its German and American counterparts, the Leopard I and the M-60A1, so there was less pressure to replace it. In addition, the British army has a much smaller budget than either of its allies, and cannot afford new battle tanks as often.

The new tank program actually started out as an export business. Britain had sold Chieftain tanks to the Iranian army beginning in 1971 as part of the Shah's army modernization program. Under the Shah, the Iranian army sought the best possible equipment, funded by a major oil boom. The Iranian army funded a further development of the Chieftain, called Shir 1, and a more radically modernized version, called the Shir 2. The Shir 2 evolved into the current Challenger.

The Shir 2 incorporated a number of major changes from the earlier Chieftain family. It was the first major British tank design to use the new Chobham/Burlington armor. It also enjoyed many automotive improvements, which gave it mobility much superior to that of the arthritic Chieftain. But the Iranian order for the British tanks was cancelled in 1980 owing to the Shah's overthrow and to the new Khomeini regime's disappointment with the performance of Chieftain tanks in combat during the war with Iraq in 1979. This was not the fault of the tanks. The Iranian armored force had been purged and many professional tankers replaced by religious zealots. In tank warfare, religious ardor is no substitute for technical experience. Several hundred Iranian Chieftains, many completely undamaged, were abandoned to the Iraqis by their amateur crews.

The British army, its budget never the best and further stretched by commitments in Northern Ireland, was in no position to spend the millions of pounds needed to design an entirely new tank. The Shir 2, modified to satisfy British army requirements, seemed like an economical alternative. The modified Shir 2 was accepted for British army service as the Challenger and entered service in 1983, a few years after the M1 Abrams and the Leopard II. The Challenger offers many of the same advantages as the M1 and the Leopard II in terms of improved mobility and protection. Ironically, it has proven to have disappointing performance in firepower, traditionally a strong suit in British tank design since World War II.

This became evident in 1987 at the Canadian Army Trophy meet. The British army expected that the Challenger, entering for the first time, would place among the top teams. The meet had been dominated in recent years by the Leopard II and the M1, with their advanced fire controls. Unfortunately, the Challenger's performance was not equivalent to that of the new German and American tanks, being more similar to that of the older generation M60A3, Leopard 1, and Chieftain. Hoping that this was just bad luck or a fluke, the British army tested other Challenger tank crews. The results were also poor compared to the performance regularly attained by M1 and Leopard II units.

The problem stemmed from the fact that the Challenger's fire control system was not a completely new design, like those on the M1 and the Leopard II, but an evolutionary outgrowth of the Chieftain's fire controls. As a result, it was not as well integrated as the American and German systems, and tank crews found it much more difficult to use. The new systems in the American and German tanks allow tank crews to locate, engage, and hit targets much more quickly than on older generation tanks. This was not the case with the Challenger. As a result, acquisition of the Challenger was terminated after about four hundred were ordered. The British army examined the M1A1, the Leopard II, and a proposed improved Challenger, the Challenger 2. Under intense political pressure, the British Ministry of Defence decided to pursue development of the Challenger 2, which could enter service in the early 1990s if the problems with the original Challenger's fire control system can be cleared up.

MERKAVA

The Israeli armored force has seen more tank combat than any other major army. Not surprisingly, many other armored forces look to the Israelis in hopes that some of their experience and battlefield successes will rub off. The Merkava is the first indigenous Israeli tank design. It is worth looking at, because it represents an approach to tank design that is radically different from that of the three premier NATO tanks we have already examined.

Israeli experience in tank design is founded on a successful program to modernize European and American tanks. In the 1950s, the Israelis bought up old World War II Sherman tanks, and with French assistance modernized them with improved 75mm and 105mm guns. The tanks were very effective in the 1967 war, even against modern Soviet tanks. Likewise, Israeli M-60 and Centurion tanks have been improved much beyond their original performance. The Merkava design was largely dictated by the expe-

The Israelis learned their own lessons from the 1973 war, and designed a tank very different from the American M1. Lacking the Abrams' advanced Burlington armor, the Israelis instead used conventional steel armor for the Merkava tank, but used a unique rear turret configuration to increase the passive protection of the crew. Israeli Government Press Agency

riences of the 1973 war and by the unique nature of the Israeli armed forces. Skilled tank crews, not the technical superiority of their tanks, have been the critical ingredient in Israeli victories. To the Israeli army, their tank crews are a commodity far more precious than the tanks themselves.

The Merkava was developed with protection as its primary requirement. The Israelis did not have access to the secrets of Burlington armor when they developed the Merkava, so they adopted a different approach to the vehicle layout. To begin with, their budget was tight. Instead of designing the tank from scratch, they decided to take the best elements from their two existing tank types: the American M-60 and the British Centurion. The power train, engine, and gun came from the M-60; the suspension was derived from the Centurion. The Israelis incorporated these elements into a new armored hull and a new turret design optimized for protection.

The engine in the Merkava is front mounted to protect the crew compartment. A hit on the hull front may penetrate the outer armor, but it has to pass through the transmission and engine before reaching the crew compartment, which is virtually impossible with the Merkava's configuration. To protect the ammunition, it was mounted in ammunition panniers in the rear hull of the tank, not in the turret as on the M-60 and the M1. The rear hull is the least likely place to be hit during tank fighting, which allows the tank to be much more rapidly reloaded with ammunition. The turret on the Merkava is well shaped to prevent penetration and is smaller than comparable turrets, such as that on the M-60. The advantages of these features were well demonstrated during fighting in Lebanon in 1982, when only a small number of Merkavas were knocked out, none in tank combat.

Although the Merkava has been widely praised in the media for its attention to crew protection, it does not compare to current NATO tanks in many respects. Its mobility is suited to the environment in which it is expected to operate: the rocky hills of the Golan Heights. But in the less severe European environment its mobility cannot equal the performance of the M1 and the Leopard II due to the limited output of its engine. The Merkava weighs more than the M1 but has only two-thirds the horsepower. This doesn't really matter to the Israeli army, since the presumption is that the tank will often fight from prepared defensive positions as it did in 1973. The front-mounted engine makes the Merkava more susceptible to power-train damage. Tanks often run into things during combat, and front-mounted drive sprockets tend to transmit the shock of such collisions into the transmission and engine. The Merkava's gun fire controls do not provide full fire-on-the-move capability comparable to that of the M1 and the Leopard II.

The Merkava is an interesting case of a tank being built under a tight budget and tailored to fit local requirements. It has not had much impact on NATO tank design. Its high level of protection can be surpassed on NATO tanks with Burlington armor without the sacrifices implied by a front-mounted engine. Israeli tank design tends to be more heavily influenced by NATO designs than vice versa. The Israelis cannot afford the expensive research and development costs associated with many tank technologies, such as fire control and ammunition, so they have remained dependent on NATO allies, especially the United States, for many advances. Locally developed improvements, as well as features available from U.S. programs, are being incorporated into the new Merkava Mark 3.

RUSSKIY TANK

How do the M1 Abrams and other new NATO tanks compare with current Soviet tanks? Actually, quite well. In nearly all technical respects, the M1A1 is equivalent or superior to the current Soviet T-80 tank. Indeed, in many categories, the M1A1 Abrams is superior. The Soviets have a tank design philosophy that is very different from that of the U.S. Army. The Soviets presume that a tank will survive only two or three battles. So they see no point in adding sophisticated features that they consider frills: thermal sights, elaborate gun stabilization systems, advanced armor. In many respects, their current tanks have the same fire control systems found in NATO tanks of the early 1970s. What Soviet tanks lack in technology they make up in numbers. The Soviets currently build about four times as many tanks per year as the United States. The U.S. has two tank plants; the Soviets have four. The U.S. has one full-time tank design team; the Soviets have two. The Soviets recognize that they may come off badly in a one-on-one tank duel, but they intend that every opposing tank will be faced by two or three Soviet tanks.

Soviet tanks are noticeably smaller than American tanks. This has often been explained as a sly Russian attempt to make their tanks smaller targets compared to bloated NATO designs, such as the M-60A1. In fact, the small size is more closely related to economy than tactics. A smaller tank is inevitably lighter. A lighter tank requires a smaller, cheaper engine, and a smaller, cheaper transmission. It consumes less fuel and uses less expensive tracks. The Soviet defense budget is limited. Since Soviet military doctrine demands tactics that accent numerical advantages as the key to victory, shortcuts have to be taken in the design to permit large quantities of tanks to be built. Soviet designs have some features that would be completely unacceptable in NATO armies. For example, a portion of the fuel is stowed in external panniers above the tracks, not within the armored hull. The Soviets feel that diesel fuel is not that much of a fire hazard, and the alternative is to carry less fuel than is deemed prudent.

Stinginess in design has definite drawbacks. First of all, Soviet tankers are noticeably shorter than their NATO counterparts. The NATO tanks are designed

Due to budget constaints, Britain's Challenger tank is an evolutionary outgrowth of the earlier Chieftain rather than a wholly new design. The mediocre performance of its fire control system compared to the Abrams and Leopard II forced a redesign in the 1990s as the Challenger 2. Michael Green

to fit the ninety-eighth percentile soldier, meaning that 98 percent of all soldiers will fit inside. The Soviet designers, to keep hull and turret sizes to the bare minimum, design for roughly a thirty-third percentile soldier; that is, for troops less than five feet seven inches tall. Even for short soldiers, Soviet tanks are very tight inside. The Soviets also use shortcuts in sound and vibration dampening. The combination of high noise and vibration levels and the tight spaces makes sustained combat actions with Soviet tanks more difficult for the tankers to endure. Arab soldiers who served in Soviet tanks during actual combat complained how rapidly crews become exhausted in tanks of Soviet design compared to those of western design.

Although there are few creature comforts on Soviet tanks, their designers do not skimp on the raw essentials of combat. Soviet tanks almost invariably have guns as big, or bigger, than standard NATO types. The current Soviet 125mm gun has been in service since the late 1960s, at a time when U.S. tanks were still armed with 105mm guns. However, the bore size does not automatically mean that the larger gun is superior in performance. Soviet tank guns generally use lower pressure gun chambers, which are cheaper to manufacture but do not offer the higher performance of the NATO gun tubes, which can take greater stress when firing. To make a long and complicated story short, Soviet tank guns do their job very well, even

The German Leopard I was a contemporary of the M60, sleeker and more agile, but less well armored.
Michael Green

52

if their larger bore size does not translate directly to higher penetration capability. The Soviets have also been adventurous in tank ammunition design, pioneering the use of armor-piercing fin-stabilized discarding sabot (APFSDS) ammunition long before it was adopted as the standard type by NATO.

Although Soviet tanks are close to NATO tanks in basic gun performance, they have serious shortcomings in fire controls. The T-72 and T-80 do not have real fire-on-the-move capability. Their guns have a two-axis stabilization system. This gives some fire-on-the-move capability, as long as the vehicle hull isn't bounced around too much, as when moving in rough terrain. The stabilization system is adequate at low road speeds, about fifteen miles per hour, and works best if the tank is moving on a relatively flat surface, such as a road. It cannot begin to compare to the systems on the M1 Abrams or the Leopard II. Much the same applies to other elements of the T-80's fire control system. The Soviets do not yet make widespread use of muzzle reference systems or crosswind sensors. As a result, their accuracy at longer ranges is less than that of comparable NATO systems.

The Soviets feel that the high-cost, fire-on-the-move systems used on NATO tanks, though desirable, are not cost-effective. These systems make the biggest difference at longer combat ranges such as 2,000 meters (1.2 miles). However, much of Central European terrain is "fine grained," that is, it has an observation distance of 1,000 meters or less. At these close ranges, fine gun adjustments made possible by muzzle reference systems and crosswind sensors don't make enough difference to be bothered with. A Soviet 125mm round will hit a target at 1,000 meters in a half second, hardly enough time for any substantial ballistic drop, or interference by crosswinds or barrel warp.

The Soviets are falling behind in night-fighting equipment. Although they pioneered it in the 1950s, they have been lagging behind as the equipment has become more and more dependent on advanced electronics. The Soviets began adopting image intensification sights in the mid-1970s, after NATO, and have

The M1A1 Abrams' closest contemporary is the German Leopard II. Although there are some differences in the designs, such as a diesel engine on the Leopard, *their combat performance is very similar.*
Michael Green

still not fielded an appreciable number of thermal imaging sights on tanks, even though these have been in service on NATO tanks for more than a decade. The problem here lies mostly with the production shortcomings of the Soviet electronics industry. The Soviets have managed to design thermal imaging sights, but they simply can't afford to build them in sufficient numbers at a reasonable price. Tanks are low on the priority list for this precious technology, with applications such as combat aircraft, warships, and combat helicopters having first priority.

A problem related to the economic bottlenecks is maintenance. As we will detail in Chapter 5, the Soviets train their tankers very differently from the way the U.S. Army does. As a result, a Soviet tank unit has far fewer experienced, professional troops than are in a U.S. Army unit. Advanced fire controls and night sights inevitably mean more frequent and more complicated maintenance tasks for the individual

Contemporary Soviet tank design places greater emphasis on quantity than on technological quality. Tanks like this Soviet T–72 have a gun similar to that of the M1A1 Abrams, but lack the sophisticated fire controls, thermal imaging sights and elaborate layered armor of their Western counterparts. Sovfoto

54

tank crews. Soviet tank crews are already having a hard time keeping up with the tank technology of the 1960s, never mind the demands of the 1990s. This leads to some reluctance on the part of Soviet army officials to include sophisticated and breakdown-prone equipment, such as thermal sights, on new Soviet tanks.

It is much more difficult to armor small tanks with some of the new protective systems than it is large tanks. Soviet tanks do not incorporate the advanced Chobham armor used on NATO main battle tanks. They appear to use a form of siliceous core armor, which consists of layers of ultrahard ceramic inside a basic shell of cast steel armor. This type of armor offers very good protection for its weight, especially against kinetic energy penetrators. But it is not as useful against shaped-charge warheads, such as anti-tank guided missiles. As a result, in 1985, the Soviets began fitting reactive armor blocks to their tanks to supplement the basic vehicle armor. We will detail the way this type of armor works in the next chapter. It is an alternative to Chobham armor, but it is not as effective in a number of respects.

Soviet tank design has slipped in quality over the past decade compared to the radically new NATO tanks. In the 1950s, the T-55 was a close match for the U.S. Army's M-48 Patton: Its gun was as effective, its armor as thick, and its fire controls not substantially inferior. In the 1960s, the T-62 compared very well to the M-60. Its new gun, with advanced APFSDS ammunition, was superior in some respects to the ammunition used on U.S. tanks of the day. Its armor was similar in effectiveness to the M-60's. And the T-64 tank, which first appeared in 1967, was superior to the M-60 and the Leopard I in most respects. Since the T-64, however, Soviet tank design has been stuck in the doldrums. At a time when NATO has been introducing a radically new generation of main battle tanks, the Soviet army has been adopting only slight, incremental improvements on their latest tanks, the T-72 and T-80. But since the Soviets are no slouches when it comes to tank design, it wouldn't be surprising to see a revolutionary improvement in Soviet tank technology in the early 1990s.

Chapter 3

Armored Shield

When the first photos of models of the XM-1 were released to the public in the 1970s, there were a lot of snickers. Radical new ideas seldom find a ready home. The XM-1's slab-sided turret defied the old verities of armor layout. Even the trade press spoke of ''poor armor layout,'' ''shot traps,'' and ''excessive bulk.'' Observers had come to expect that modern tanks would have sleek, well-rounded turrets,

After suffering grievous losses to enemy infantry firing antitank rockets in the 1973 war, the Israelis developed an antidote in the form of explosive reactive armor. The armored boxes on this M60A1 tank explode *when a rocket's shaped-charge warhead explodes against them, disrupting the formation of the penetrating jet of the enemy warhead.* Israeli Government Press Agency

better able to deflect the blows of tank rounds. In contrast to the elegant cast turret of the British Chieftain and the Israeli Merkava, here was a tank with a turret that looked like a child's clumsy attempt with Lego blocks. When pictures appeared of the XM-1's German counterpart, the Leopard II, the same strange design was again evident. Had the tank designers in America and Germany all gone nuts?

Burlington armor was completely secret at the time, and for a few years no one beyond a small circle of designers knew what had caused the sudden change in the shape of tanks. But Burlington armor was only one of the radical new ideas incorporated into the XM-1 Abrams. The Abrams tank finally passed its trials and in 1981 was accepted by the U.S. Army as standard equipment. The *X* (for experimental) was dropped from its name, and it became simply the M1 Abrams. (The army also decided around this time, due to the increasing use of computers, to drop the hyphen from military designations, so the M-60A1 tank became the M60A1.)

Explosive reactive armor was first used in the 1982 Lebanon war on tanks like these M60A1 tanks in the outskirts of Beirut. It was effective though hardly foolproof. Israeli Government Press Agency

In many respects, the technological advance in the M1 over the older M-60A1 was as great as the leap from propeller-driven fighters to jet fighters. The changes covered the whole range of capabilities: speed, protection, gun accuracy, crew protection, even maintenance. These new features came at a price. The M1 was about 30 percent more expensive than the current M60A3, and more than 50 percent more expensive than the older M-60A1. Two million dollars is a lot of money to spend for a tank, no matter how capable it is. But foreign designs, such as the German Leopard II and the British Challenger, were even more expensive.

The engineers designing a tank have to work within a strict "weight budget," in the case of the M1, a bit under sixty tons. More armor protection means that weight savings have to be made in the power plant or the suspension. The M1 design team, headed by Dr. Phillip Lett, had crew survivability as the top priority. It was the army's reading of the lessons of the 1973 war, combined with assessments from computer models of the likely shape of future wars in Europe, that survivability of the tank would be the key. The army presumed that U.S. tankers would be fighting outnumbered, so keeping the tank and its crew in the struggle as long as possible was an essential element in winning the battle.

Usually, protection is thought of simply as armored protection. This was certainly the case in older tanks. The designers thought that placing a lot of steel on the front of the tank would be enough to protect the crew. In the M1 Abrams, the approach is very different. Armor, especially the new Burlington/Chobham-style armor, is a central ingredient in protecting the tank. But other elements are important as well, such as preventing onboard fires, limiting the likelihood of catastrophic ammunition fires, and making the tank more agile to avoid enemy missile teams.

One of the criticisms leveled against the M1 is that its side and rear armor is too thin. On a television news magazine program, one of the investigative reporters stood in front of an M1 holding a Soviet RPG-7 antitank rocket launcher, claiming that this hundred dollar weapon could destroy a two million dollar tank. Is this possible? Yes. But is it probable? No.

The layout of tank armor is based on probability. Tank designers have to answer the question, What weapon, fired from what angle, is most likely to knock out tanks most often? Based on this judgment, they allot a percentage of the armor to different portions of the tank. No single tank is equally armored all around. For example, in the older M-60A1 tank (which is not as strictly classified as the M1), the front of the tank is protected by steel armor that is more than 150mm (6 inches) thick. The turret sides are about 75mm (3 inches) thick and the rear is thinner still. The front armor is sufficient to resist the 100mm gun on the older Soviet T-55 tank. The side armor might be sufficient to protect against a 100mm projectile if it hit the armor at a glancing angle. But a direct impact would cut through the armor. If the M-60A1 had its entire structure armored with six-inch-thick steel, it would weigh more than 200 tons—fine for an immobile pillbox but not a healthy weight for a tank. If, on the other hand, the M-60A1 was limited to its current weight but the armor was distributed equally all around the tank, the frontal armor would probably be about three inches thick—not enough to stop a typical World War II tank projectile, never mind a modern antitank projectile.

Accepting these constraints, how do the designers decide where to put the thickest armor and where to place the thinnest? It's a mixture of common sense, tradition, and computer studies. From studying historical records of knocked-out tanks, some general assumptions can be made about where tanks are most often hit. The most common are hits to the front of the turret and the front of the hull, and hits on the side from frontal angles. Hits from the side come in a close second. Finally, rear shots are the least common. So, armor tends to be thickest in the frontal quadrant, which means the front of the turret and the hull, and in the portions of the turret and the hull side most likely to be hit by frontal shots. This is not simply a matter of following the cold logic of operational research and computer analysis; a certain amount of tradition is also involved. Tankers have always been trained to use their tanks with the front to the enemy, even when withdrawing. The thicker frontal armor is used like a shield, always pointed at the enemy.

The thickness and type of armor selected are based on the type of weapons most likely to knock out a tank. In the case of the M1 Abrams, special attention was paid to defeating shaped-charge weapons. There are basically two approaches to knocking out a tank: kinetic energy (KE) and chemical energy (CE). Kinetic energy weapons are projectiles that bore through the armor using a combination of mass and speed. An ordinary bullet is a KE penetrator. In the arena of tank fighting, the most common KE penetrator today is the APFSDS projectile. American tankers call these rounds sabot, whereas Russian tankers call them hard cores. The sabot projectile looks like a big dart. Its main body is smaller in diameter than the main gun, so it has a metal or composite "sabot" around it to fit properly in the gun tube. When the

The Soviets payed close attention to the Israeli use of reactive armor and received samples courtesy of the Syrians. Later in the 1980s, Soviet tanks began to sport similar armor, seen here on a Soviet T–80BV tank.

projectile is fired, the sleeve falls off after the projectile leaves the gun tube, and the dart continues on to its target. Modern APFSDS projectiles weigh about twenty pounds and impact at speeds of about one mile per second—in other words, with about the energy of a truck hitting a wall at sixty miles an hour but concentrated in an area the diameter of a dime! Not surprisingly, it is very difficult to protect against this sort of weapon.

Chemical energy projectiles work in a different fashion. As the name implies, these projectiles rely on chemical energy, high explosives more precisely, to bore through the armor, rather than the sheer brute force of the KE projectile. There are several different types of CE antitank projectiles. Ordinary high-explosive artillery rounds don't work very well against

armor. When they explode, they expend their force almost equally in all directions, so there is not enough energy in any one direction to blast through the armor. Tankers used to employ a round called squash head, or HESH (high-explosive squash head), which delays the detonation of the high explosive momentarily to allow the explosive to build up against the armor plate. The explosive then detonates, with somewhat more force going in a frontal direction. The squash head explosion is not enough to actually blast through the armor, but it can knock a big flake of steel (called spall) off the inside face of the armor, which then ricochets around the inside of the tank with very nasty results. The problem with squash heads is that certain types of layered armor can easily defeat them.

The most common CE warhead, and indeed the most common antitank warhead, is the shaped charge, also called hollow charge, since the volume in front of the cone is empty. The shaped charge, as its name

The British approach to the antitank-rocket problem has been passive armor. In the 1980s, older British Chieftain tanks received a layer of secret Stillbrew armor, believed to be a package of steel armor with an internal layered core of ceramic and other materials. Terry Gander

The most effective protection to date against the threat posed by high explosive warheads in Chobham armor, also known by its codename Burlington. It was first developed in Britain, and is now used, in improved form on the American Abrams and the German Leopard II tank. Shown here is a British Challenger I tank, the first British tank to employ the new armor. Terry Gander

implies, consists of high explosive shaped around a copper cone. The shaped-charge effect has been known for almost a century, but it was first used in antitank weapons in World War II. When the shaped charge hits the tank, the explosive is detonated. Much of the energy is concentrated forward and blasts the thin copper cone into a concentrated high-velocity jet of metallic particles, which bore a narrow hole through the steel armor. This ability to concentrate the explosive force in a narrow stream makes the shaped-charge warhead a very efficient tank buster.

The shaped-charge warhead is common because it is so simple to deliver against a tank. A KE penetrator, such as the sabot, has to be fired from a large, heavy gun to be effective against tank armor. Since its action depends on mass and velocity, man-portable antitank weapons with KE penetrators are virtually impossible. In contrast, a shaped-charge warhead does not have to be fired at high speed to do its deadly work. In fact, speed has little effect on its penetrating abilities, and slower speeds are preferable. Therefore, a tank gun isn't needed to fire them; a simple little

The U.S. Army studied Israeli reactive armor but developed an improved type. It is used only by the U.S. Marine Corps; the army preferred to spend its money on more M1 Abrams tanks. U.S. Army/DoD

rocket motor will do fine. Shaped-charge warheads also are amazingly destructive for their small size. In older generation weapons, the rule of thumb was 4 : 1 cone penetration ratio. This technical gobbledygook means that the warhead will penetrate to a depth of four times its cone diameter. So, a typical antitank rocket grenade, with a cone diameter of 85mm, will penetrate 340mm of steel armor, more than thirteen inches. And this warhead will weigh only a few pounds! New warheads have cone penetration ratios of 7 : 1, and experimental types using new metal liners such as uranium promise 15 : 1. This means that a small infantry antitank rocket grenade can punch through the thickest conceivable steel armor.

What are so worrisome to tank designers are the small size and ease of delivery of the shaped-charge weapons. The KE penetrators, such as sabot, require big guns, such as those on tanks. So it's not likely that there will be any sudden upsurge in the numbers of these types of weapons on the battlefield. But advances in shaped-charge technology in the 1960s meant that weapons using shaped charges were suddenly appearing all over the place in rapidly escalating numbers. The old Soviet RPG-2 rocket grenade launcher of 1950 could penetrate only a few inches of steel and was so large that only one infantryman in fifteen could carry one. Today's RPG-22 can cut through more than twelve inches of steel armor and is so compact that every infantryman can carry one.

Shaped charges are also used on the deadly antitank guided missile. The problem with infantry rocket-propelled grenades is that it takes courage to use one.

The slab-sided appearance of the German Leopard II tank is a dead giveaway that it is protected by the new Burlington-type armor. This layered, nonsteel armor has evolved to the point where it is nearly impenetrable by current antitank weapons. Michael Green

Sure, it can cut through twelve inches of steel. But it has to be fired from only a few hundred feet to be likely to hit the tank. Few infantrymen have the composure to stand up to a clanking sixty-five-ton tank bearing down on their foxhole at forty miles an hour. The lone infantryman knows that much of the time the little antitank grenades won't knock out the tank. But they will make the enemy tank crew more than a trifle annoyed and draw unwanted attention in the infantryman's direction. These grenades typically have cheap fuses, so they don't always detonate. If they hit at a glancing angle or hit an unimportant part of the tank, they don't do much damage. Even if they do hit a vital section, the warhead may just barely penetrate the tank's armor, and there won't be enough energy left in the shaped-charge jet to do any serious damage inside the tank.

The bigger antitank guided missile gets around this problem in a number of ways. First, the missile can be fired from a long distance, typically 2,000 meters (1.2 miles). At that range, a tank will have a hard time seeing the soldier firing the missile. Contrary to widespread belief, an antitank missile's back blast is not very visible, especially if seen from more than a mile away. The blast lasts only a fraction of a second, and during the day it is difficult to see unless the observer is either quite close to the launcher or is looking directly at the blast. So it doesn't take exceptional courage (or rash foolishness) to use a weapon such as this against a tank. The guided antitank missile also uses a larger warhead. Typical unguided antitank rocket grenades, such as the legendary RPG-7, have a 73mm warhead, whereas a typical antitank guided missile has a 150mm warhead, nearly twice as large. This means that if it hits the tank, it has a much better probability of both penetrating the armor and inflicting lethal damage.

It was this type of weapon that led to the demise-of-the-tank stories after the 1973 Mideast war. The weapon in question was the Soviet Malyutka (AT-3 Sagger) antitank missile. The Malyutka is a second-generation wire-guided missile. It is compact and has a nasty warhead. But it is very difficult to use. The operator looks through a little periscope and then steers the missile over the wire-guidance link using a portable joystick control. This requires tremendous eye-hand coordination, since the operator is trying to track the missile by spotting its rear-mounted flare, while at the same time keeping track of where the target tank is. It requires considerable practice and a cool head under combat conditions. The Malyutka caused about 10 percent of Israeli tank losses in 1973, although dozens of missiles were fired for every hit.

The Malyutka was worrisome enough to tank designers, but what was more worrisome was the next generation of missile. The first of these to appear was the American TOW (tube-launched optically-tracked wire-guided) missile, and similar European and Soviet missiles soon followed. These also use wire guidance but a much more ingenious guidance system. These systems have a tracker inside the launch post, which automatically follows the flight path of

The success of the M1A1 Abrams in the Gulf War was due in no small measure to vigorous testing before the war that uncovered problems and fixed them before the vehicle entered production. Shown here is an overhead air-burst test to determine the protection afforded to the tank when under artillery fire. U.S. Army/DoD

Protection is not only armor, but stealth as well. To hide a tank from enemy observation, smoke has been the traditional means as is seen in this sequence showing a smoke grenade pattern exploding over an M1 Abrams. What is different in the new generation of tanks is that they can see through their own smoke using their thermal imaging sights, while the enemy often cannot see them. Steven Zaloga

the missile. The missile operator has only to superimpose the cross hairs of the launcher sight on the image of the enemy tank and the launch system automatically sends guidance corrections along the wire to the missile. Unlike the Malyutka generation of missiles, which took dozens for a hit, the new generation, such as TOW and Milan, has a demonstrated combat kill rate of better than one for every two launches.

So what does all this mean for the tank designer and the armor package of the tank? When the M1 was being designed back in the early 1970s, a revolution in tank busting was going on. In 1950, a Soviet tank division had about 250 weapons with a high tank-killing capability (most of these being tank guns). They also might have had a few hundred RPG-2 rocket grenade launchers, but with a very low tank-killing

A pattern of smoke grenades burst over an M1 Abrams. During Desert Storm, smoke grenades were not very necessary since the poor weather con- *ditions often provided their own cover to U.S. tankers.* Michael Green

probability. Soviet rifle divisions of the time, the most numerous type of Soviet army division, had even less tank-killing capability. By 1970, with the advent of the RPG-7 and the Malyutka generation missile, things were changing. Even a motor rifle division had considerable tank-killing potential. A motor rifle division with BMP infantry vehicles, for example, would have 250 tanks with high tank-killing potential, more than 170 missile launchers with a medium degree of tank-killing potential, and more than 600 RPG-7s with low tank-killing potential. What was especially alarming was that by the 1980s, the same motor rifle division had 250 tanks with high tank-killing potential, more than 300 new generation AT-4/AT-5 antitank guided missiles with high tank-killing potential, and 3,000 rocket grenade launchers of various types, with low (but improved) tank-busting potential. So we see a jump from about 350 antitank weapons in 1955 to 1,000 in 1975 to 3,500 in 1985. And virtually all of this jump comes from weapons with shaped-charge warheads.

Gilbert Harvey's invention of Chobham/Burlington armor came at a most auspicious time. Burlington armor is designed primarily to repel shaped-charge warheads. Although its inner configuration is still a secret, it appears to work by breaking up the hypervelocity jet of metal particles used by the shaped charge to bore through armor. Layered armor is not new. In World War II, layered armor was used by the Germans against older types of kinetic energy penetrators, such as hardened cap projectiles, since it was found that the projectiles broke up after passing through layers of armor. Burlington armor is quite thick, almost two feet on the M1 Abrams, although much of this is probably air or a lightweight filler. What presumably happens is that the hypervelocity jet, on entering the Burlington armor, is deflected by the different layers of metallic and nonmetallic materials, losing its precious energy all the time. The first generation of Burlington armor is reported to be the equivalent of 750mm (30 inches) of steel armor, whereas the improved BRL armor used on the newer IPM1 and M1A1 is equivalent to about 1,000mm (40 inches) of steel armor. A typical contemporary shaped-charge warhead, such as the Soviet AT-4 Spigot, has a penetration of about 500mm (20 inches) of steel armor, so these new armors are quite effective.

The contest between warhead designers and armor designers continues. The M1 armor package was designed with a heavy emphasis on defeating shaped-charge weapons. The basic steel armor behind the Burlington armor is capable of stopping the Soviet 115mm kinetic energy round. But Burlington armor was not originally configured to deal with larger threats such as the current Soviet 125mm gun or the forthcoming 135mm gun. The added armor on the IPM1 and M1A1 will probably defeat the current Soviet 125mm APFSDS round (which can penetrate about 450mm of normal steel armor). In the mid-1980s, the U.S. Army's Ballistics Research Lab developed a more advanced type of Burlington armor that incorporates a special depleted-uranium mesh in the array. This new armor, first used on later production M1A1s, will stop the Soviet 125mm round and gives the tank protection equivalent to about 600mm (24 inches) of steel armor—an awesome amount by anybody's standards. A tank commander compared the protection afforded by the M1 to the older M-60: "You can't compare the survivability of this with the M-60. If I went in with a '60, I'd feel as safe as if I were in a submarine made out of screen doors."

The effectiveness of the M1A1's new armor package was made abundantly clear during Operation Desert Storm. No fewer than seven M1A1s took direct hits, mainly from the 125mm guns of T-72s, and suffered no penetrations or crew casualties as a result.

REACTIVE ARMOR

Passive armor, such as steel and Burlington armor, is not the only way to protect the tank against the shaped-charge menace. In the mid-1970s, German engineers at MBB (the modern descendant of the legendary German aircraft firm Messerschmidt, combined with other German aeronautical firms, such as Blohm) came up with the idea of reactive armor.

As bizarre as it may seem, reactive armor involves the use of explosives to defeat the shaped charge. The explosives are contained in small boxes, sometimes called bricks or tiles, which are used to cover vulnerable parts of the tank. Inside each box is a sheet of metal, backed with a sheet of plastic explosive. When the box is struck by a shaped-charge warhead, the explosive is detonated, which throws the metal drive plate, or disruptor plate, into the path of the shaped-charge jet, greatly reducing its penetrating abilities. The plastic explosive is insensitive to small-caliber kinetic energy projectiles (such as machine gun bullets).

Reactive armor was ignored by NATO tank designers for a variety of reasons. Because of its use of explosive, it can damage nearby portions of the tank and injure unprotected crewmen and troops nearby. Reactive armor also requires that the plate be hit within a certain zone of angles for the best protection. If the reactive armor block is hit from odd angles, it doesn't have much protective effect. Although Burlington armor accomplishes the same results as reactive armor and also has other advantages, the configuration of Burlington armor makes it difficult to fit to old tanks with cast turrets.

The main advantage of explosive reactive armor (ERA) is that it can be retrofitted to older tanks. This made reactive armor very attractive to the Israeli army, which apparently became aware of it through the patents issued to MBB engineers. The Israeli de-

Small details help make a tank more effective. On the M1 Abrams, the commander's hatch can be locked overhead, allowing him the advantages of all-around natural vision while at the same time protecting him from air-burst artillery. Steven Zaloga

fense development group Rafael developed a version of reactive armor called Blazer, which was used to equip M48, M60, and Centurion tanks that took part in the 1982 war in Lebanon. The Blazer armor offered a measure of protection to the tanks but was not entirely successful. It added a considerable amount of weight to the tanks and was not entirely reliable. In the past few years, the Israelis have begun to replace the Blazer armor with a new passive applique armor using layers of steel and ceramic. The modified M60s, called Magach, look very different from their original American examples.

The Soviets were working on a similar system for their own tanks. The smaller size of Soviet tanks and the tight constraints of the Soviet defense budget made a Soviet version of Burlington armor less attractive than other alternatives. Instead, the Research Institute of the Main Armored Force at Kubinka, outside Moscow, developed its own version of ERA. In 1982, the Syrians captured an Israeli M48 with Blazer ERA and turned it over to the Soviets. The Soviet team at Kubinka found that it confirmed their own research, and in 1985 Soviet tanks in East Germany began to be fitted with reactive armor. This came as a shock

Tanks are not equally armored all around, otherwise they would be too heavy. The tank must be intelligently employed by its crew to exploit its strong points and protect its weak points. A tradi- *tional tactic of tankers since World War II is hulldown, using terrain features to minimize the visibility of the tank, and its vulnerability to enemy fire.* Steven Zaloga

to many western observers, since it decreased the capabilities of NATO's large inventory of guided anti-tank missiles.

The appearance of reactive armor has led to a technological arms race between Soviet tank designers and NATO missile designers. (A similar race is probably also taking place with Soviet missile designers as they try to develop countermeasures for Burlington armor.) New generations of NATO antitank guided missiles, such as the TOW-2A and Milan 2T, can defeat reactive armor using a concept known as tandem charge. A small shaped charge at the tip of the missile detonates the ERA brick microseconds before the main shaped charge is detonated. The disruptor plate is largely out of the way before the main shaped-charge jet is detonated. The Soviets are now trying to counter this by using passive appliques, such as the Israeli Magach steel/ceramic armor, or by adding additional layers of ERA tiles. Of course, NATO then tries to counter these moves with top-attack warheads, which explode over the thin roof armor of the tank and evade the reactive or passive armor panels altogether. And the contest goes on and on.

The NATO decision to go with Burlington armor has avoided much of this technological turmoil. Burlington armor is not as simple to defeat as reactive

There is also protection in mass. The mobility advantages of the M1 with its powerful engine allows field commanders to rapidly mass forma- *tions and overwhelm the enemy with speed and concentration.* Michael Green

armor and has proven more durable in the face of rapid technological change. The U.S. Army had its own reactive armor program for the older M-60 tanks but decided against adopting it. The consensus was that most forward deployed divisions in Europe and Korea would have the M1 anyway, and the money would be better spent on more M1s. A reactive armor kit costs about $100,000, which is nothing to scoff at in times of tight defense budgets. A small number of applique armor kits were manufactured and have been fitted to U.S. Marine Corps M60A1 tanks since 1989 as a stopgap until the planned arrival of their M1A1 tanks. Four of the five Marine tank battalions in the Desert Storm Operation still used the old M60A1, and only a fraction of them had this appliqué armor kit.

SURVIVABILITY

Armor is the best-known, but not the only, means to protect a tank. Tanks can also be designed to limit the amount of damage if they are penetrated. And features can be incorporated to reduce the likelihood of the tank being hit in the first place.

No matter how good the armor, penetration of its thinner portions is always possible. The tank designer has two concerns when facing the prospects of tank penetration: protecting the crew and preventing catastrophic loss of the tank. Tanks are not like combat aircraft. When an aircraft is shot down, it is totally destroyed. Tanks can be knocked out and recovered, and live to fight another day. Indeed, in prolonged wars, it is not unusual for tanks to be knocked out several times and be returned to battle. Catastrophic tank loss—that is, a tank loss where the tank cannot be recovered or rebuilt—is usually due to propellant fires. Previously, for example in World War II, there were two causes of catastrophic loss: gasoline fires and propellant fires. These days, the use of diesel fuel reduces the likelihood of fuel fires, since diesel fuel does not ignite as readily as gasoline.

Propellant fires are dangerous for a variety of reasons. The propellant in a round of tank ammunition must contain its own chemical oxidant to detonate properly in the tube of the tank gun. The chemical contains its own supply of oxygen, which means that it is nearly impossible to stanch the fire by usual means. When the propellant is ignited, it burns fiercely and usually ignites nearby rounds of tank ammunition. The interior of the tank is then engulfed by a violent storm of searing flames. The tank doesn't actually explode; rather, each round of ammunition is split open by the heat and its propellant is ignited in a great woosh of fire, much like a rocket engine. There is virtually no chance for the crewmen in the tank to survive unless they bail out of the tank before it is engulfed in flames.

Tanks such as the M1 Abrams have a fire protection system using Halon gas. But this is intended to smother other types of fires, such as those caused by hydraulic fluid leaks, rather than enormous, self-sustaining fires, such as propellant blasts. The NATO tanks' designers have approached the propellant fire hazard in different ways. On the British Challenger, the ammunition is contained beneath the turret ring. The expectation is that the ammunition is far less likely to be hit low in the hull, so fires are less likely to be started.

The U.S. Army's M1 Abrams and the German Bundeswehr's Leopard II take still another approach. Most of the ammunition is placed in the rear of the turret, but it is compartmentalized. On the M1 Abrams, the ammunition is located behind special, hydraulically operated blast doors. When the loader needs a round, he opens the door with a lever, and then the door shuts. If the rear of the turret is penetrated by an antitank missile and the ammunition is set afire, the blast door prevents the fire from spreading into the crew compartment. The fury of the fire is directed away from the crew compartment by special blast panels in the roof. The detonation of the ammunition blows these panels open, so the intense jets of burning propellant vent upward through the roof openings rather than inward at the crew. This is the first generation of tanks to seriously attempt to limit the effects of propellant fires on the tank crews.

The many burn casualties suffered by the Israeli tank force in 1973 led to other changes as well. Tanks such as the Abrams and the Leopard II are fitted with automatic fire control systems. The Abrams's Halon fire-extinguishing system contains an electrooptical sensor that detects the intense heat of a turret penetration within microseconds of its occurrence. This triggers a high-pressure Halon extinguisher, which smothers any fire in less than a blink of an eye.

Aside from propellant fires, the ignition of hydraulic fluid is the most common cause of crew burns. Hydraulic fires are far less likely in the M1 Abrams than in the M60 due to its higher level of armor protection and the careful attention paid to minimizing the likelihood of major ruptures. As an added precaution, American tank crews are now issued Nomex coveralls, which have been used by aircrews and other troops for a number of years and are much more fire resistant than normal battle dress.

The other method to avoid tank destruction is to keep from being hit in the first place. The U.S. Army's selection of the AGT-1500 turbine was due in part to a desire to give the tank much quicker acceleration

Speed is another form of protection. A moving tank is much more difficult to hit with either a missile or a tank gun than a stationary tank. American tank *tactics stress the use of speed and agility in defeating opposing forces.* Michael Green

and higher cross-country speed. It might seem bizarre to suggest that a few extra miles per hour of road speed can help a tank outrun a missile traveling at near-supersonic speed, but that is exactly the case. The tank is not actually outrunning the missile; rather it is complicating the aim of the missile gunner. Unlike a tank gun, which hits its target about a second after the trigger is pulled, the missile gunner must continue to guide his missile for ten to fifteen seconds after the missile launch. At ranges of 1,500 to 2,000 meters (1 to 1.2 miles), a tank is a tiny blob in the sight of a missile operator. A tiny blob jinking around in the sight is a much more difficult target to engage than a stationary blob.

The same applies to tank versus tank fighting, especially at shorter ranges. Soviet tanks are poorly provided with stabilized fire control systems and have a hard time tracking rapidly moving tank targets. The closer the range, the greater the relative angle of change of the targeted tank in the gunner's sight. This was very evident in Operation Desert Storm. American M1A1 tanks were able to engage Iraqi T-72s at ranges over 2,000 meters. The Iraqi tanks, although theoretically capable of reaching these ranges based on their gun performance, could not effectively engage the M1A1 Abrams due to the limitations of their fire controls. Furthermore, when attacked by M1A1s on the move, they were ineffective even at shorter ranges.

The rapid acceleration possible with a turbine permits innovative new combat tactics. Ideally, tanks engage enemy tank formations from a hull down position. Hull down means that the tank is protected by terrain features or entrenchments so that only the gun and the top of the turret are exposed. When a tank fires from a hull down position, it becomes very apparent to enemy tankers. Although it might hit one enemy tank, other tanks in the formation will spot it by the enormous flash of the gun and by the amount of lingering dust kicked up in front of the tank's position by the gun's blast pressure. With a turbine engine, the M1 Abrams tank can rapidly accelerate immediately after firing, moving in either forward or reverse gear away from its initial position before the enemy can respond. Diesel-engined tanks can make use of the same tactics, but since their acceleration is so much slower, they are not as agile from a cold start.

It is a popular adage that offense is the best defense. In the next chapter, we will take a look at the impressive changes that have taken place in modern tank guns.

Chapter 4

The Sharp End of the Sword

At first glance, the M1 Abrams does not seem to offer much of an advance in firepower over its predecessor, the M-60A1. Both are armed with the standard NATO 105mm gun. But appearances are deceiving. Although the guns are much the same in both tanks, the M1 Abrams's new fire control system is a revolutionary departure from all previous generations of tanks. It allows the tank to fire on the move with as much accuracy as the M-60A1 firing from a stationary position. And its thermal imaging system allows it to fight at night as well as in the daytime. Its ballistic computer and sensors give the gun long-range accuracy that was possible in the past only with expensive missiles.

Until the advent of the Abrams and other tanks of the new generation, such as the Leopard II, tanks basically fired from the halt. Move, stop, shoot. Move, stop, shoot. Not surprisingly, the most advantageous tactic for tank fighting was a well-protected entrenchment where the tank could sit and fire away, most of its bulk protected by earth. But movement is another way to protect a tank. It is much more difficult to hit a tank on the move than a stationary tank, especially in rolling terrain where its motion is unpredictable.

For a long time, attempts have been made to give tanks fire-on-the-move capability. Warships have the same basic problem, since the motion of the sea makes it essential to somehow stabilize the gun. No matter how much the ship rocks, the guns must remain aimed at the same fixed point. The problem with tanks is their relatively small size; even a small warship's

gun turret is larger than an entire tank. Size is no concern in the design of warship gun stabilizers, and they have been around for a century. Warship gun stabilization systems, however, are much too big to fit into a tank.

The first attempt to develop a tank gun stabilization system took place in World War II. The American M-4 Sherman tank had a rudimentary gyrostabilizer; it was the only tank of its generation to incorporate such a system. The consensus among tankers was

Muzzle blast! Modern tank guns kick out a tremendous amount of flash on firing. Greg Stewart

that it didn't work very well, and so it wasn't often used. Indeed, American tankers disliked the system so much that the first generation of postwar American tanks, the M-47 and M-48, weren't even fitted with it. The first successful attempts to provide stabilization came in the 1970s, mostly as retrofit programs for existing tanks such as the M-60A1 and the Leopard I. These systems stabilized the gun and the related sights in two axes. Although this didn't give the tanks a real fire-on-the-move capability, since disturbances in the third axis would throw off the gun (two-axis stabilization covers gun elevation and gun traverse;

the third axis is the cant of the gun trunnion), the main advantage of these systems was that the gunner could keep his eye on the target more easily than with previous unstabilized gun systems, so that when the tank did halt to fire, the halt was very short.

Tanks of the new generation have their guns and gun sights stabilized in all three axes: elevation, traverse, and cant. With the stabilization system turned on, the gun barrel and sights remain trained on exactly the same point no matter how the hull moves. This makes it possible, for the first time, to fire even while moving through rough terrain. Combined with the

The enormous muzzle blast of modern tank guns is a problem in dry desert terrain, since enormous clouds of dust make it difficult to determine whether or not the target has been hit. This is alleviated on newer tanks by the presence of new thermal imaging tank sights. U.S. Army/DoD

high cross-country speeds of current tanks, it becomes much more difficult for an enemy tank gunner or an enemy missile operator to keep the tank in his sights and aim accurately.

Firing a tank gun at targets one mile away takes considerable precision. It's not simply a case of hitting the tank but hitting its most vulnerable part. A turret that is just a fraction of a degree off will miss an enemy tank by many feet. Hydraulic or electric turret traverse systems must move a twenty-ton turret with the precision of a finely tuned watch.

Other factors affect tank gun accuracy as well. Modern tank gun projectiles use fin stabilization to keep them moving in a straight path. The problem with finned projectiles is that they can be disturbed by crosswinds. A crosswind can blow a projectile several feet from its intended target, and the problem becomes more and more serious the farther away the target is located. The M1 has a wind sensor mounted on the rear turret roof; this feeds data to the tank's ballistic computer, which takes into account such disturbances when aiming the gun.

The length of modern tank gun tubes creates another problem. The longer the tube, the better the projectile exploits the energy given off by the gun propellant. In other words, a longer tube will fire out a projectile at a higher speed, so the projectile will penetrate more armor when it hits the enemy tank. But long

During peacetime training, the use of a simulator is more common than the use of actual ammunition. Real ammunition costs in excess of $500 per round, *and crews only get to fire about 100 rounds a year. Soviet crews, however, seldom fire as many as ten a year!* Marlene McGinnis/Video Ordnance

tubes can warp from repeated firings, which can throw off the aim of the gunner. A slightly warped tube will cause a shot to miss by more than a yard at a range of a mile.

The problem of gun tube warpage has been solved in two ways. You will notice in the photos that the M1 Abrams has covers over the gun tube. These are called thermal sleeves. They insulate the tube from dramatic temperature differences, e.g., between the air temperature and the barrel temperature, to reduce warping. If you look carefully, you will notice a small device mounted above the muzzle opening. This is a muzzle reference system, which is connected to the gun fire control system and automatically feeds data about barrel warp to the ballistic computer.

The other key bit of information that the tank's computer needs to properly adjust the gun is the distance to the target. Range doesn't make much difference in close-range combat. But at distances of more than a thousand yards, the projectile drops due to the pull of gravity. The computer can compensate precisely for this dip by elevating the gun a degree or so, depending on the exact range.

There are a variety of ways to determine range. A stadia range finder, used on many older Soviet tanks, consists of a series of small graticules that are etched into the gunner's sight and look like a small ruler. By placing the graticules over the image of the enemy tank, the gunner can estimate its range by how much space it takes up in the graticules. Obviously, a tank only a few hundred yards away will take up more space in the sight than one that is a mile away. This method is not very accurate, since enemy tanks are seldom so obliging as to appear ninety degrees head-on. They appear at varying angles, making the range estimation less precise.

Since the 1950s, many tanks have used optical range finders, which work in much the same way as modern single lens reflex cameras. With the target in the sight, by focusing the sight, the range can be determined. Until the 1970s this was the standard method of range estimation with tanks such as the Leopard I and the M-60A1. Although more precise than stadia range finders, this system has drawbacks.

It isn't that precise at longer ranges, where accurate readings are most important. And it doesn't work as well when the light is poor or when the enemy tank is obscured by dust.

The main advance in range finding came with the advent of lasers in the late 1960s. Lasers emit a precise beam of light of a single frequency, and they can be mated to a detector. When the laser is beamed at a target, some of the light is reflected back; this beam can be picked up by the detector. The laser beam can be sent out in coded pulses so that the detector doesn't mistake random light for the laser beam. This process is extremely rapid, since light travels at more than 186,000 miles per second. The laser range finder system determines the range within inches by timing the beam from the precise moment of emission to the time microseconds later when the reflections return.

All of these systems can be added to older tanks to improve their fire controls. The M60A3 is fitted with a laser range finder, wind sensor, and thermal sleeve. The Leopard 1A5 has had many of these features added as well. The new generation of tanks, such as the Abrams, is the first to have these features fitted from the outset. This is important, since it allows the whole fire control system to be carefully integrated to take maximum advantage of these advanced features.

It is often wrongly assumed that this complex array of features makes modern weapons more difficult to use. Newspaper accounts frequently complain that modern weapons are getting so complex that every soldier needs a college degree in electrical engineering. In fact, the opposite is the case. A pocket calculator is technologically more complex than a slide rule or an abacus but is much easier to use. A well-integrated fire control system, such as the one on the M1 Abrams, is considerably easier to use than the older fire control system on the M-60A1. A tank commander with the 67th Armor, the first unit to be equipped with the M1, recalled: "When I first saw the tank, I thought it was too complex. I took one look inside the turret, saw all that high tech stuff, and thought, Wow, is this tank ever going to be hard to learn. But after I trained on it and studied it, it wasn't. It looks complicated, but anyone can handle the simplified computer.''

The U.S. Army conducted a test to compare the M1 gun system with the older system on the M-60A1. On the average, the gunners on the M1 did more than 45 percent better: The brightest crews scored 25 percent better, and the troops in the lowest mental category scored 85 percent better.

The M1 gun system also allows the crew to engage targets faster, since the system is easier to use. For example, during the 1985 Canadian Army Trophy meet, the M1 Abrams crews took only ten seconds on the average to engage a target, whereas M60A3 crews took fourteen seconds. Not only were the M1 crews faster, they hit their targets 93 percent of the time, compared to 77 percent for the M60A3 crews.

These advances might seem trivial, but they are not. It's not the improvement in peacetime scores that matters; it's the effect on wartime performance. Tank combat is a grueling, stressful business that can easily lead to nervous exhaustion. A complicated

The tank projectile contains a small tracer at its base which helps the tank crew trace the flight path of the projectile, as seen in this night firing view. Night *tank fighting was very common in Desert Storm because of the use of thermal imaging sights on the M1A1 Abrams tank.* U.S. Army/DoD

fire control system that requires a well-trained crew in peacetime becomes impossibly convoluted to men suffering from too little sleep and too much stress. Judging from the results obtained during Desert Storm, the advances in fire controls have been worth the expense.

THE GREEN EYE

The other big change in tank fighting is the thermal imaging sight, sometimes called a FLIR for forward-looking infrared. The thermal imager is as big an advance in tank fighting as radar was in air combat. It allows the tank to fight at night much more easily than with any previous night-vision system. And it even improves the ability to fight in the daytime.

In World War II, the standard way to fight at night was to call in artillery illumination. The artillery would fire illumination rounds, which would burst over the battlefield. Bright flares dangling beneath a small parachute would bathe the battlefield in an eerie glow. The problem was that the lighting was erratic, it didn't last long, and it made both sides equally visible to each other. By the end of the war, both the Germans and the Allies were working on new night-vision sys-

In the 1960s, the U.S. Army attempted to improve tank-gun accuracy by developing guided missile rounds for tanks, as in the case of the 152mm system on the M-551 Sheridan. This was not very successful. U.S. Army/DoD

The traditional projectile for tank fighting in the 1960s was HEAT—high-explosive antitank, seen here being loaded into an M60A1. In the 1970s, *APFSDS, or sabot for short, became the main type.* U.S. Army/DoD

tems using infrared light, which is not visible to the human eye, although it is possible to build special sights that convert infrared light into an image visible to the naked eye. The system requires a powerful searchlight to illuminate the battlefield. In 1945, the Germans began fielding their first night-fighting tank units. The units had an armored half-track with an infrared searchlight, and the tank crews had their own infrared viewing devices, called metascopes. The Ger-

Modern tank ammunition is heavy and cumbersome, even this 105mm HEAT training round. Some armies are going to autoloaders to solve the problem. Steven Zaloga

man night tank units entered the war too late to have much effect. One battalion roughed up a Soviet tank unit during the fighting in Hungary in the winter of 1945, but that was the extent of their impact.

After the war, most armies experimented with infrared night-fighting equipment. The Soviets, having learned the hard way what such equipment can do, were the most enthusiastic advocates. By the mid-1950s, most Soviet main battle tanks had their own infrared searchlight and suitable night-vision devices. The NATO countries followed suit but with less vigor. There is a major problem with night-fighting systems that rely on searchlights: If both sides have metascopes, the side that first turns on its searchlights is in trouble. The searchlights may be invisible to normal eyesight, but through a metascope each is as bright as a full moon. Any tank using its searchlight becomes a juicy target for the other side.

Infrared night-fighting systems have been used in combat, but usually when only one side has them. For example, in the 1973 Mideast war, the Israeli tank units on the Golan Heights faced a serious threat on several nights when the Syrian forces had infrared equipment and they did not. They called in artillery illumination, but the battle was much tougher than usual.

In the 1960s, American electrical engineers developed the first practical passive night sight. Passive sight means that it does not need to emit any form of light or other radiation to create an image. This sight was based on a new technology called image intensification. The sight resembles a video camera, and it collects the minute amounts of moonlight and starlight that are present on all but the darkest nights. The sight then amplifies the signals to present a television image to the gunner. These sights are often called starlight sights, since they do need a certain amount of natural light to function properly.

The early sights had problems. They were so sensitive that bright flashes of light, such as tank guns firing, caused the imaging tubes to become overloaded and "bloom." The gunner's screen was completely filled with light, and it took several seconds before the screen returned to normal. This was not a very helpful feature in a viewing system intended to be used with a tank gun. It obscured the target precisely when the gunner was trying to determine whether or not he had hit the target. The other problem, of course, was that the sights needed light to function properly. The sights typically work under conditions of at least "a sixth moonlight," meaning ambient light equal to one-sixth of a full moon.

The spoilsport in all this is cloud cover. In Europe, there is nighttime cloud cover many months of the year, especially in winter and fall. Cloud cover blocks natural light, so there is nothing for the image intensification sight to see. This might not render starlight sights completely ineffective, however, since man-made light, such as fires and artificial illumination reflecting off the clouds, would substitute for moonlight.

Improvements in image intensification sights cured the blooming problems and also reduced the amount of natural light needed to create a useful image for the tank gunner. These improved sights were first adopted in large numbers on NATO tanks of the mid-1970s and are still one of the most common forms of night-fighting equipment. Usually, tanks fitted with these sights still carry infrared searchlights in the event there is insufficient natural light due to cloud cover.

The real breakthrough came in the mid-1970s with the development of thermal imaging. Infrared sensors have been around for many years. They can pick up the differences between natural objects by the differing levels of heat energy (infrared) that they give off. This is the principle behind infrared guided missiles, which sense the difference between the hot engine exhaust of a jet fighter and the rest of the natural background. For many years, it was possible to use special infrared films, which formed their images using infrared energy the way that normal photographic films use visible light. Thermal imaging systems were an improvement over film, since they viewed images in real time and did not require any form of chemical processing. And they were an advance over earlier infrared missile seekers, since their greater sensitivity could provide an actual image of the object being viewed, not simply a blob of light on the display.

Thermal imaging is an especially important concept for tanks. It is one of the few advanced electronic sensors that can be used in ground combat. Ground surveillance radars so far have not proved practical for imaging pinpoint targets. Thermal imagers can easily pick up the targets of greatest interest to tank gunners—other tanks and vehicles. Man-made objects usually give off more heat than the natural background

Modern tanks carry both sabot and HEAT ammunition as is the case here with this German Leopard II tank. (The cutaway round is sabot). Each has its own role: sabot for tank fighting, HEAT for other targets. Michael Green

79

of plants and soil. For example, a tank engine heats up not only the rear of the tank but much of the hull and turret. Even if a tank is stationary all day, the large metal hull acts like a big heat sink, soaking up the sun's energy. At night, the tank gradually gives up this heat, which is then visible to the thermal imaging system.

Unlike the active infrared searchlight system of the 1950s, the thermal imager is completely passive. It doesn't give off any energy of its own, which would be visible to enemy gunners. And unlike image intensification sights, it does not need ambient starlight or moonlight to function, since it sees energy that exists even on pitch-black nights. This makes the thermal imager the first truly effective night-fighting sensor for tank combat.

Thermal sights were first used on improved versions of older tanks. The M60A3 tank was retrofitted with a thermal sight, becoming the M60A3 (TTS). This is currently the most advanced version of the M-60 family in U.S. Army service. The M1 Abrams was the first main battle tank to incorporate the thermal sight in its design right from the outset of production.

Thermal sights are not without drawbacks. They are very expensive, often costing as much as a quarter million dollars, about a tenth the total cost of the tank. The early systems broke down frequently and required serious maintenance. But these sorts of problems are typical of any revolutionary new system and have gradually lessened as the technology matured. One of the reasons the thermal sights suffered so many breakdowns is that they were being overused. The thermal sight had been developed primarily as a night sight to replace the earlier image intensification sights. What tankers soon discovered was that the new sights are useful in the daytime as well. To understand why this is the case, we must first take a look at why tank sighting devices are so important.

Finding the enemy tank first, before he fires on your tank, is a vital tactical advantage. American studies of tank combat in Korea found that in cases where U.S. tanks spotted the North Korean tank and fired first, the kill ratios were between 16 : 1 (for M-4 Shermans) and 33 : 1 (for M-26 Pershings). That means that in such circumstances, at least sixteen enemy tanks were knocked out for every U.S. tank lost. In contrast, when the North Korean tanks found the American tanks first, there was a less than fifty-fifty chance of the American tank surviving. Finding the enemy first is one of the key ingredients in successful tank combat.

It is obvious how the thermal sight helps find the enemy at night. But what about in the daytime? Tanks are not easy to spot even in full daylight. An enemy tank, in a hull down position, covered with natural camouflage with only the top of its turret showing, is very difficult to see with the naked eye. But infrared energy passes through the camouflage, making the tank visible through the thermal sight. In addition, the modern battlefield is apt to be obscured by dust and smoke, which armies regularly use to veil their movements. Thermal sights can see through most smoke and dust, peeling away the veil to reveal the target. A tank with a thermal sight can find targets in the daytime more quickly than a tank without such a sight.

Use of the thermal sight also permits novel tactics. Presume, for a moment, a company of M1 Abrams tanks encountering a company of Soviet T-72 tanks during the daytime. The M1 has a thermal imaging sight; the T-72 does not. If the M1 Abrams company fires its smoke grenades, the T-72 company can no longer see them. The T-72s are blind. But the M1 company can see through the smoke cloud, making the T-72s still vulnerable to their fire. This advantage will be lessened, however, with the advent of new types of smoke grenades capable of blinding thermal sights.

During Operation Desert Storm, thermal sights provided one of the most important technological advantages that the United States forces held over their Iraqi opponents. The Iraqi forces, using mainly Chinese and Soviet tanks, had no thermal sights. The Iraqis did manage to obtain several thousand image-intensification sights from the Dutch Delft firm. These were retrofitted to some T-62s and T-55s. Iraqi T-72s with the Republican Guards had Soviet image intensification sights. But as mentioned before, image intensification sights, while better than nothing, are not as versatile as thermal sights. The weather during Desert Storm did not favor image intensification sights because there was cloud cover during nearly the entire period of the ground war, blocking out from the battlefield the moonlight and starlight needed by the Iraqi sights.

In contrast, the American M1A1 Abrams tanks, fitted with thermal sights, could easily locate and destroy Iraqi armored vehicles long before the Iraqis even knew that the American armor was present. Critical technological advantages such as these are one of the reasons so few American tanks were hit during the tank fighting in Iraq and Kuwait.

SHARPENING THE SWORD

The main advantage of the M1 Abrams over earlier tanks is its sophisticated fire controls. But its gun has been improved as well. The M1 Abrams's main armament is the M68A1 105mm cannon, essentially the same as the M68 version on the M-60 family of tanks. The improvements have not been made to the gun itself, but rather to the ammunition.

In the 1960s and 1970s, the preferred ammunition for tank-vs-tank fighting was HEAT (high-explosive-antitank), basically a tank version of the shaped-charge warhead used in antitank guided missiles. Because HEAT offered better armor penetration than the kinetic

Loading ammunition is one of a tank crewman's many chores. Besides the many technological changes in tank ammunition, one of the other *obvious changes has been the substitution of aluminum cases for the ammunition in place of the older and more traditional brass cases.* U.S. Army/DoD

energy rounds of the day, it was preferred. For example, the kinetic energy penetrator for the 90mm gun of the M-48 Patton tank could pierce about 160mm of steel armor, compared to more than 200mm for the HEAT round for the same gun. The problem with HEAT is that the projectile has poor ballistic performance at long ranges, tending to drop more rapidly than sleeker kinetic energy rounds.

The other disadvantage of HEAT is that its behind-armor effects are often not as deadly as a kinetic energy penetrator. It's not enough to simply penetrate the armor of the tank; the projectile must have enough energy left to do serious damage inside the tank. When a shaped-charge warhead breaks into a tank, it creates an overpressure wave that can debilitate the crew even if they are not struck by the jet of metal particles that sprays into the tank, causing dam-

age and starting fires. A kinetic energy round often breaks up during penetration; large fragments of intensely hot metal enter the inside of the tank and are far more likely to kill the crew, smash open ammunition racks, and start deadly propellant fires. The incandescent metal fragments spray into the tank like a shotgun blast and ricochet around the inside of the tank until their energy is expended. This creates a gruesome effect if it happens in the crew compartment.

In the 1973 war, a new type of kinetic energy projectile was used for the first time, the APFSDS, also called sabot ammunition (mentioned previously in Chapter 3). This type of ammunition was pioneered by the Soviets. Previous types of kinetic energy projectiles had been shaped like conventional bullets. The sabot rounds are narrower and are shaped like finned darts. The destructive power of a kinetic energy pro-

Loading ammunition in peacetime is laborious. The real worry is that current tanks carry so little, only 40 rounds compared to about 80 in World War II *tanks. So, means to more rapidly reload a tank are being devised, including ammunition cassettes.* U.S. Army/DoD

jectile is dependent on the mass (weight) of the projectile and the speed at which it impacts the target. Due to the laws of physics, increases in velocity increase the impact energy and penetrating power more effectively than increases in projectile weight. By sacrificing weight for speed, APFSDS dart projectiles proved to be more destructive than earlier forms of kinetic energy projectiles. Their lower weight permits higher impact velocities, and they are ballistically more efficient due to their streamlined shape.

The original Soviet sabot projectiles were made of ordinary steel. The early American sabot ammunition had a tungsten carbide core, which is denser and a more efficient penetrator. By the late 1970s, a new material was being tested for sabot rounds—depleted uranium. A by-product of nuclear power technology, it consists of isotopes of uranium with little radioactivity remaining. It is an extremely dense metal, heavier even than lead, which makes it a very useful metal in penetrators where high weight per volume is desirable. Tungsten carbide penetrators for the 105mm gun can penetrate about 350mm of steel armor, compared to about 420mm for the newer depleted-uranium types, such as the M833 projectile. Depleted uranium also has one other interesting property from a military standpoint. High-speed impact between uranium and steel causes the shattered bits of depleted uranium to become pyrophoric, meaning that they become incandescent, like a child's sparkler. This increases the destructive effects when a depleted-uranium projectile penetrates a tank.

The U.S. Army is one of the few armies to use depleted uranium for ammunition, and it is often given a euphemistic name—staballoy. European armies, especially the Bundeswehr, are reluctant to use this material because of public apprehension over anything that smacks of nuclear weaponry. In fact, the main problem with depleted uranium is not any residual

The increase in tank firepower over the past decade has not been so much in the growth of gun tube size, but rather in the accuracy of the new tanks due to their integrated fire-control systems and computers.
Greg Stewart

radioactivity, which is minor, but chemical toxicity. Like lead, depleted uranium is a hazardous heavy metal that can cause serious poisoning if particles are inhaled or swallowed. It is difficult to machine and handle as a result.

BIGGER GUNS

The German Bundeswehr decided to adopt a 120mm gun right from the outset for their new Leopard II tank. Greater gun caliber does not automatically ensure greater armor penetration. Indeed, the U.S. Army was reluctant to part with the 105mm gun, feeling that ammunition improvements and other changes (such as a lengthened gun tube), rather than increased caliber, could lead to penetration improvements similar to that possible with the new Rheinmetall 120mm

gun. Nevertheless, the U.S. Department of Defense pushed for adoption of the German gun to ensure greater commonality between the two allied armies. The U.S. Army and the Bundeswehr have by far the largest tank forces of any of the NATO armies on the central front. The British army proposed a new gun for the improved M1 as well. But ammunition commonality with the British army of the Rhine is less effective, since German tanks substantially outnumber British tanks in NATO.

At first, the new German 120mm ammunition did not offer substantially better armor penetration than the most advanced varieties of 105mm ammunition. But the larger bore diameter does offer long-term potential. The current M829 APFSDS round is estimated to be capable of punching through 525mm of steel armor at standard combat ranges, and it is predicted that the experimental XM946 round will be

This is the easy way to engage targets—from the standstill. But new generations of tanks such as the   *Abrams can engage accurately while on the move.*
Steven Zaloga

84

able to smash through an incredible 900mm (32 inches) of steel. Keep in mind that battleships have only about sixteen inches of steel armor!

The tank's main gun is its primary weapon, but not its only one. The M1 Abrams also has three machine guns. These include a coaxial 7.62mm machine gun alongside the main gun, an M2 (Ma Deuce) .50-caliber remote-control machine gun above the commander's station, and a 7.62mm M240 machine gun on a ring mount over the loader's hatch.

The M1 Abrams is the first American tank in thirty years not to have the commander's machine gun cupola. This had been a standard (and fairly unique) feature of American tank designs since the M-48A1 tank of the mid-1950s. The idea was to permit the commander to use his machine gun from under the cover of armor.

Combat experience demonstrated that these little subturrets were not a good idea. The Israeli tankers considered them to be a hazard to the tank commander, especially the very large type fitted on the M-60. To begin with, the cupola projects more than a foot above the rest of the tank. Even when the tank is fighting from hull down, the cupola is exposed to hostile tank fire. When hit with a tank round, the cupola tends to be ripped off the turret with unpleasant results for the tank commander. The Israelis, as well as many other tank veterans, have long argued that the tank commander has to have his head outside the tank during combat to best see what is happening and to pick out targets. These subturrets make that difficult, and put the commander in a high and vulnerable position. To make matters worse, the M85 machine gun in the turret is not the most popular machine gun in service, especially compared to the reliable Browning .50-caliber M2.

The Israelis solved the problem on the M-48A2 and the M-60A1 by removing the machine gun cupola and replacing it with a simple Urdan cupola patterned after the one on the original version of the M-48 tank. The machine gun is attached on a pintle mount, which makes it easier to use at close ranges. The U.S. Army followed suit when rebuilding its M-48s into the new M48A5 model for the National Guard.

It stopped using the machine gun subturret and adopted the Israeli cupola. Unfortunately, the M60A3 still has the machine gun cupola. The army has been reluctant to ask for funds to modernize the M-60 family beyond the M60A3 effort, preferring to divert the money for the purchase of more M1s.

The M1 and M1A1 have a simpler commander's station than on the M-60. It uses the more reliable .50-caliber M2 heavy machine gun, which can be fired from inside the tank by remote control. The hatch has an interesting feature: It can be locked in a partially open position over the commander's head, which allows him to keep his head outside the tank for observation, while providing overhead cover from artillery airbursts and other mayhem. The commander's cupola on the M1 Abrams has not proven to be entirely popular, however. Many tankers find the fixed mounting for the .50 caliber awkward to use, particularly when engaging close-range targets. This feature is being redesigned for the future M1A2.

There had been debate about the secondary armament for the Abrams when the tank was still in the design stage. Some World War II veterans were pushing for grenade launchers in place of the M2 Browning. But grenade launchers don't have the range of machine guns, and their ammunition takes up much more space. Thought was also given to mounting a coaxial 25mm Bushmaster cannon in place of the 7.62mm machine gun. Although this was viewed with considerable favor at the time, it would have added considerably to the cost and complexity of the design, and was dropped for these reasons.

These machine guns might seem to be useless decoration, considering the awesome firepower of the 120mm gun on the current M1A1 Abrams. Veteran tankers are of a very different opinion. The M1A1 carries only about forty rounds of main gun ammunition—too little to be wasted on suspected enemy positions. During World War II, American tankers quickly learned the value of prophylactic fire. When approaching unknown territory, a few bursts of machine gun fire could often help to discover a tank-hunting team squad behind the foliage or an antitank missile team lurking in an abandoned building. The Israelis learned the same lessons from their combat experiences, and it is not surprising to see that Israeli tanks are festooned with far more machine guns than NATO tanks. Israeli tanks typically have a machine gun over every hatch.

The Merkava even has an additional .50-caliber machine gun over the main gun, in addition to the coaxial machine gun. And the Israelis also provide the Merkava with a small mortar.

One of the more interesting efforts studied by the U.S. Army was the addition of Stinger antiaircraft missiles to the sides of the M1 Abrams turret. Machine guns are very useful in dealing with ground targets but not so effective against aircraft and helicopters unless used in heavy concentrations. A Stinger missile pod could provide self-protection to the tank. This idea hasn't caught on yet, but it may eventually be considered in future tank designs.

This combination of improvements in ammunition, fire controls, and turret stabilization greatly increases the lethal firepower of the new generation of tanks. These features extend the effective combat range of modern battle tanks to more than 2,000 meters. The addition of thermal sights gives them true day- and night-fighting capability for the first time. But in the end, the effectiveness of a weapon system is dependent on the troops who use it. Next, we will look at the human element of tanks.

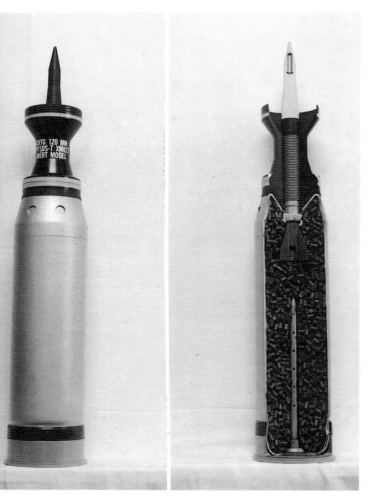

In the end, tank combat comes down to putting the projectile on target. This cross section shows the standard M827 120mm sabot ammunition of the M1A1 Abrams tank. The dart-shaped projectile is made of depleted uranium and is surrounded by a black sabot which peels away once the projectile flies out of the gun tube. U.S. Army/DoD

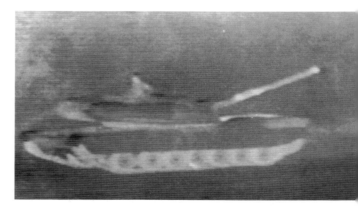

During Desert Storm, the thermal imaging tank gun sight proved to be the most critical new innovation in tank technology. The Iraqi tanks didn't have this advantage. Iraqi tanks could be spotted through smoke, rain, haze and dust. According to tankers who were there, with the thermal sight, it wasn't combat, it was a shooting gallery. U.S. Army/DoD

Chapter 5

Tanker

Few things are as exhilarating as charging across wide open fields at forty-five miles per hour in the turret of an M1 Abrams tank. With the stabilized gun seeking out its target with pinpoint precision, the turbine whining at high speed, the tank seems like an unstoppable force. Major Doug MacGregor, an armor officer, reflected on tank duty:

There's nothing comparable to serving on a tank. There's a certain rush that comes with moving across open country with a large number of tanks. . . . The wind against your face. You have this sense of irresistible power. The sense that there's nothing out there that can stop you. Whether that's true or not is irrelevant. The point is that, psychologically, when you are in a tank, you believe that you are irresistible, beyond destruction. And, of course, that's a tremendous psychological advantage. Which means that the shock action and the impact of a tank force is likely to be very great. Because the soldiers believe in it.

But tanking is not an old man's sport. It is physically grueling to an extent that becomes apparent only after a few days' hard bashing.

Tank duty is not for the claustrophobic. A tank is not very spacious inside, and it seems even more compressed when the hatches are closed. The driver in an M1 has only a little more space than he would in a coffin. The turret is roomier, depending on the type. The M-60A1 seems almost cavernous compared to the M1 Abrams. The interior is painted white to better reflect what little light is in the turret when the hatches are closed. Tank designers try to make the insides "user-friendly," but no matter how hard they try, riding in a tank going cross-country at top speeds is a bit like taking a tumble in a clothes dryer. The M-60's interior decorator seems to have settled on plumbing as a design motif. The interior of the M-60A1 has all the charm of a boiler room. The M1 Abrams is much the same, except that the gunner's station has a dash of Star Wars thrown in by the computerized fire control system.

Tanks inevitably operate in rough terrain. No matter how good the suspension, hitting a ditch at thirty-five miles an hour is going to be a jolting experience for the whole crew. The loader, who stands up to move the ammunition, is thrown forward into the electrical control boxes in front of his station. The gunner, with his face pressed against the brow pad of the gunner's sight, has his head banged against the sighting controls. The commander, if riding outside the tank, gets his ribs smashed into the hard steel edge of the turret opening. Padding is kept to a minimum in tanks—padding burns. Black-and-blue bruises are part of the trade.

The tanker's uniform is basically the same as any other soldier's uniform. There is no special padding. The only concession to safety is a combat vehicle crewman (CVC) helmet. The CVC is smaller than the normal steel pot, or "fritz" helmets, worn by other troops. The new version is much more compact than the "bone dome" version from the 1960s and 1970s. An additional purpose of the CVC is to insulate the crew from the deafening sound of a moving tank.

The turbine engine is behind a thin steel firewall only inches behind the turret crew. The gun makes an ear-shattering crack when fired. The tracks give off a deafening shriek when moving at top speed. In fact, the sound inside a tank is so loud that you feel it rather than hear it. The CVC helmet muffles the noise so that it is loud rather than deafening. The CVC also links the crew through the intercom system. It is too noisy to communicate without the intercom. One of the first things etched into a tanker's brain as a reflex reaction is to hit the switch for the mike when he wants to speak to other members of the crew.

In spite of all the talk in the media about "gold-plating" modern weapons, there is very little in the way of crew comforts in modern tanks. The interior of the M1 is ruthlessly functional. Whatever doesn't add to the efficiency of the tank's mission isn't included in the design. For example, there is a refrigeration system for the thermal night sight but no air-conditioning for the crew. In hot weather, the inside of a tank is baking hot. One concession to crew com-

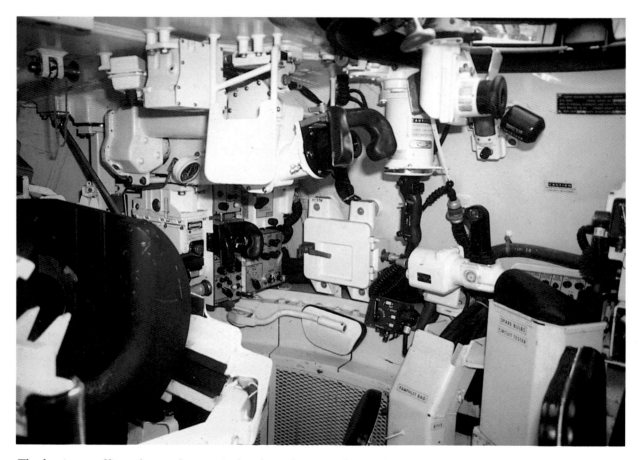

The business office of a modern main battle tank. This is the right side of the turret inside an M1 Abrams tank. The black object to the lower left is the gun breech, the sights in the center of the picture are operated by the tank gunner. Steven Zaloga

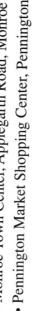

...tion of tanks,
...t the first thing
...s winter.
...to the armored
...tucky, nestled
...sville. It's best
...ne of the U.S.
...tankers as the

...nove on to ad-
...ches them the
...e four crewmen
...ner, tank com-
...how to perform
...ner, and driver.
...they will most
...osition, that of
...l crew members
...l the essentials
...they can move
...ally, tank com-
...nented: "Tanks
...the only piece
...the people and
...u have a four-
...to the outcome
...at machinery."

serves of ammunition, called semiready, one at his feet and one behind the commander in the right side of the hull. Once the main compartment is exhausted, the loader uses these.

Loading the main gun requires practice and stamina. Current tank ammunition is quite heavy, about fifty-five pounds, and is also cumbersome. The space the loader occupies is about the size of a small closet. Loading the gun isn't difficult when the tank is station-

There is a distinct hierarchy in the four-man tank crew. The loader is usually the most junior member of the crew since his responsibilities are the most straightforward. While inside the tank in combat, he loads the tank gun from ammunition magazines in the rear of the turret, to the left. This is inside an M1 Abrams tank. Steven Zaloga

loader. After a recruit finishes advanced individual training, he is usually assigned to a tank battalion. Being the most junior member of the crew, he will probably be given the position of loader. This job does not require the skill or experience of the other three positions, so it falls to the least experienced. As the name implies, the loader's primary responsibility is to load the main gun. The loader's station is in the left side of the turret. The main ammunition storage area is the rear turret bustle, behind the loader. Called the ready ammunition, this is the first place the loader goes to select ammunition. There are two other, smaller, reary, but it becomes very challenging when moving. The gunner has a small seat, but the loader needs to be on his feet to get the kind of leverage necessary to load the tank ammunition. Although the torsion bar suspension absorbs some of the blows of cross-country travel, it is still a bumpy ride when standing. It's something like trying to stand up in a small boat in choppy water—except, of course, that you are trying to delicately load a fifty-five-pound round into a tiny opening in the moving breech of a gun!

The loader is instructed by the tank commander (usually called TC) which type of ammunition to load.

There are usually only two choices: sabot for APFSDS kinetic energy rounds, and HEAT for high-explosive shaped-charge rounds. The loader opens the blast doors of the ready ammunition compartment by using a clever knee control. When he hits the knee control, the door is opened by hydraulic pressure, thereby leaving both his hands free. Then he swivels around to place the round in the breech of the gun, and pushes the round home with his knuckles. As the round is rammed home, it triggers the breech block, slamming it shut. Pushing in the round with his fists prevents his fingers from being mashed by the closing

The senior members of the tank crew are the gunner and tank commander. The gunner, to the left and in front, aims the main tank gun at targets selected by the tank commander behind him. The tank com- *mander, or TC, must communicate with other tanks and keep his eyes out for enemy forces. This is inside an M1 Abrams. Steven Zaloga*

90

breech block. The gun breech has an ejection guard fitted to it; during loading, the ejection guard swings free of the breech. With the round in the chamber, the loader pulls the ejection guard to the left. He then shouts ''Up'' into the mike on his helmet, which signals the other crew members that the gun is ready to fire.

The ejection guard is placed to prevent a crew member from being too close to the breech when the gun fires. It recoils with enormous force and could easily crush an arm or leg. The gun will not fire with the guard in the open position. When the guard is closed in the firing position, a yellow ''armed''

light goes on at the turret crew stations to alert the turret crew that the gun is ready to fire.

The loader has many other responsibilities beyond his main duty. During road marches, the loader mans the 7.62mm M240 machine gun that is located on a ring mount around his hatch. The loader is usually responsible for keeping air watch to warn the crew of approaching enemy aircraft. In addition, he keeps an eye over the rear quadrant of the tank for enemy troops.

The loader has responsibilities also in operating the tank while on the move. For example, it is his task to make sure that the crosswind sensor is locked

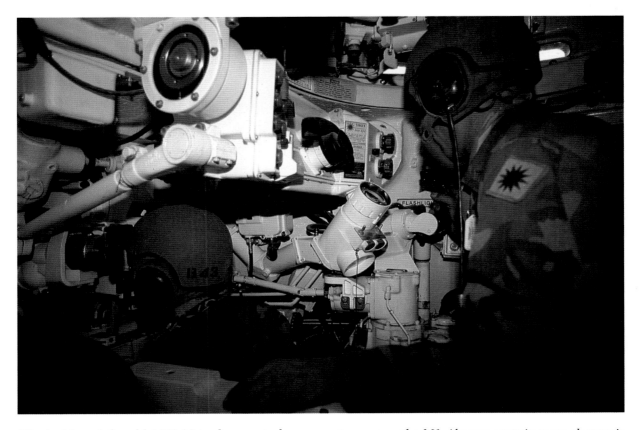

The insides of the old M60A1 tank seem to have plumbing as their decorative motif. The old fire-control systems were mechanical, while newer sys- *tems as on the M1 Abrams contain more electronic components.* Michael Green

91

into position when the main gun is being used. And the loader takes part in the many maintenance chores needed to keep a sophisticated machine such as the M1 Abrams operating. A main battle tank is not like the family car, which can operate for months with little more attention than an occasional refueling. Tanks take hours of daily maintenance. Track tension must be checked to prevent the track from coming off and the track end connectors must be tightened after every halt. Engine filters must be cleaned to allow enough air into the engine. Fluid levels must be monitored to prevent equipment damage. The suspension has to be checked to make sure that wheel hub lubricant levels are sufficient.

The load of daily maintenance chores is one of the reasons many armies have resisted fitting automatic loaders into tanks. The U.S. Army had an autoloader fitted in the abortive MBT-70 tank, and many other armies have designed them as well. But armies with combat experience, such as the Israeli army, have firmly opposed dropping the loader. They feel that three men cannot keep a tank operating properly in combat conditions. The three remaining crewmen would have to take over the chores now performed by the loader. If one of the three crewmen were wounded, there would be no reserve. Now, at least, if the loader were injured, the commander could carry out the loading tasks. This would not be an ideal

While on road march, the commander and loader ride outside the turret. The commander does his usual job of searching for the enemy while the *loader is responsible for manning the vehicle machine gun and keeping an eye out for enemy aircraft. This is a German Leopard I crew.* Michael Green

92

situation, but the tank could still operate. This debate will undoubtedly continue for many years.

GUNNER

The gunner sits in the right side of the turret, in front of the tank commander. Next to the tank commander, the gunner has the most demanding job. He is responsible for the main gun and the many subsystems associated with it, such as the vision systems, fire control equipment, and coaxial machine gun. When preparing the tank for action, the gunner must perform a preparation ritual akin to that of jet pilots. The thermal imaging system (TIS) must be turned on and cooled down for several minutes before it works properly. The turret hydraulic drive has to be checked to make sure it has sufficient pressure to function. The fire control system has a built-in test system, which has to be examined to make certain all the components are working. A computer data test is carried out to make certain the computer is entering data properly. The gunner's primary sight (GPS) has to be focused. The gun's alignment, called boresight, must be checked.

The gunner is surrounded by a bewildering number of switches and gauges. Most are used for fine adjustments of the instruments or for checking the status of the many subsystems in the turret. The gunner's basic controls consist of the GPS, which he uses to aim the gun, and the turret hand controls. The hand controls are usually called Cadillacs. No relation to the car, the nickname comes from the name of the U.S. firm that specializes in turret fire control and stabilization systems, Cadillac-Gage. The Cadillacs control the elevation and depression of the gun as well as the traverse of the turret. By tilting the Cadillacs forward, the gun points down; by pulling back, the gun elevates. Likewise, by turning right, the turret traverses right; turning left, the turret swings left. The Cadillacs also contain palm switches to fire the main gun or the coaxial machine gun.

The GPS system allows the gunner to aim the turret. The gunner can select from a daylight view or a FLIR thermal image. The GPS has two sighting options: 3X power, used for general observation, and 10X power, for identifying targets and aiming the main gun. The gunner also has a backup optical sight in case the main GPS system goes down.

The decision to engage a target is made by the commander, not the gunner. The tank commander identifies the target to the gunner, then through the intercom tells the loader which type of ammunition to use. The gunner sets a switch on the console immediately below the GPS to the proper type of ammunition. This permits the computer to make the correct change in gun elevation. The ballistic flight path of a sabot round is different from that of a HEAT round. The sabot flies an almost flat flight path, whereas the bulky HEAT round has a more arced flight path due to its less streamlined shape. The computer compensates for this by elevating the gun slightly higher for a HEAT round than for a sabot round. The computer already has other data stored in its memory, such as barrel warp, ammunition temperature, and crosswind speeds.

To aim the main gun, the gunner places the cross hairs and reticle of the GPS immediately over the point on the target he wishes to hit, using the Cadillacs. The last bit of information needed by the computer is the range to target. The gunner fires the laser, and the range pops up in the GPS. At the same time, the data is automatically fed to the computer, which can then determine how much elevation is needed to compensate for the type of ammunition, the range, and other factors. To fire the gun, the gunner squeezes the palm switch of the Cadillacs.

Firing the main gun in the M1 is a good deal easier than in older tanks. On the M-60A1, the commander had to determine the range using an optical range finder. The computer then provided a fire solution, and the gunner made final aiming corrections. This took more time than the system on the M1 and didn't allow any of the subtler corrections, such as crosswind drift and barrel warp.

One of the most remarkable changes between the M1 Abrams and the M-60A1 is the turret stabilization system. With the M1's stabilization system turned on, the gun remains aimed at one point regardless of the movement of the hull. If the driver turns the tank, the turret drive automatically compensates, keeping the gun pointed at the original position. This has a curious effect inside the tank when riding in rough terrain, since the gun breech keeps moving up and down while trying to keep the gun level to the target, although the stabilization system is turned on only when engaging a target.

The gunner is the crewman most familiar with the essential operations of the tank. Tank commanders are usually chosen from the ranks of experienced tank gunners. A few of the most talented tank gunners are selected to take a special course for master gunners.

The course helps to further develop their skills and prepare them for passing on the best techniques to other gunners in their battalion. New advances in fire control systems have made it possible for inexperienced gunners in an M1 to hit targets as readily as experienced gunners in the M-60A1. But to use the capabilities of the new tanks to the full extent, practice and training are essential.

TANK COMMANDER

The TC is the team leader in the tank. His responsibilities are not as technical as the gunner's or as physically

The most isolated member of the tank crew is the driver, who sits up in the front of the tank by himself. Michael Green

94

demanding as the loader's. But he has to know how to do all of the other jobs on the tank, besides his own, to make certain that the members of the team are performing their jobs properly. Major Doug MacGregor emphasized the qualities needed in a tank commander:

When I commanded a tank company, my preference for tank commanders, in sergeants and young lieutenants, was someone particularly alert. You want someone who is very intelligent; this is not a job for someone who is slow-witted. . . . The tank commander has to have the reaction time of a jet fighter pilot. With a minimum of guidance, in a very fluid environment, he must make decisions that can be critical to the survival, to the success or failure, of the entire mission. He's got to be tough. He's got to have perfect eyes. . . . And he's got to be physically robust. Because you spend day after day up in that hatch— you're not sitting down, you're moving day and night relentlessly. You get very little sleep. And when you add to the standard beating that you take when you move in the vehicle, the sort of maintenance tasks that go with the vehicle itself, you've got to be tough.

It might seem that a tank commander's job is superfluous. He doesn't aim the gun, load the gun, or drive the tank. He simply sits there and controls the action. In the past, many armies felt this way. French tanks involved in the 1940 war with Germany had

Essential dress for all drivers is a pair of goggles. Tanks kick up a tremendous amount of mud, dust and grit while traveling. Michael Green

only a single man in the turret who combined the roles of commander, gunner, and loader. The German tanks, with three-man turret crews, consistently outfought the French tanks. Soviet tanks in the battles of 1941 had two men—a gunner and a commander who doubled as loader. The German tanks outfought them as well. German tankers who took part in these battles remarked that the enemy tanks seemed to be confused. The tank units did not act in a coordinated fashion. They did not seem able to pick out targets very quickly or best exploit the terrain.

The reason was simple. The tank commander in the French and Soviet tanks was burdened by too many other responsibilities. He could not pay attention to what the other tanks in his unit were doing, or instruct the driver to best use terrain features to hide his tank, because he was preoccupied with keeping the gun loaded. Although the commander's job may not seem essential in the operation of the tank itself, his duty is a vital one in tank combat, where one tank must interact not only with enemy tanks but in coordination with the tanks of the same unit.

In the M1 Abrams, the TC sits in the rear right side of the turret, behind and slightly above the gunner. The commander spends most of his time with his head outside of the tank, coordinating the actions of his tank with those of the other tanks in his platoon and keeping an eye out for enemy activity. He has

Before live-fire exercises, loading the tank with ammunition is the first step. Tank crews, unlike aircraft crews, do most of their own servicing and munitions work. Michael Green

96

by far the best view of the surrounding terrain. Even when the tank is buttoned up in combat, he has vision ports surrounding his station, which give him 360-degree coverage. The tactics of the tank are directed by the TC. He selects the terrain and instructs the driver to best avoid exposing the tank to enemy fire. And on contact with enemy forces, he directs the target to engage and the type of ammunition to use.

The TC's equipment is not as elaborate as the gunner's but is sophisticated by past standards. The commander has a sighting unit that allows him to see the same thermal imaging views as the gunner. The TC can also control the turret traverse, so that when he finds a target, he can swing the turret in its general direction, while allowing the gunner to do the fine aiming.

Tank commanders are selected from the ranks of experienced gunners. By the time a tanker is selected to be a TC, he has a thorough knowledge of all the features and skills needed to operate a tank.

DRIVER

The driver is the fourth crewman of the Abrams. He is alone in the front of the tank, isolated from the rest of the crew. The driver station in the M1 Abrams is unlike any previous tank's. The driver doesn't so much sit in his seat as lie back into it. When the driver closes his front hatch and cranks back his seat, he is almost lying down. When driving the tank with his head outside the hatch, he can adjust his seat to a more ordinary position.

The unusual configuration of the driver's seat was selected to keep the overall height of the M1 Abrams as low as possible. The height of the hull is usually determined by the seated height of an average adult. By angling the seat, precious height is saved. The seat is not the only novel feature in the driver station of the M1 Abrams. There is no steering wheel but a steering yoke that looks as though it belongs on a lawnmower.

The yoke is actually more like motorcycle handlebar controls, without eighteen inches of handlebar

in between. The M1 has an automatic transmission, so shifting is controlled by a small lever at the center of the yoke. The handlebars on either side of the yoke twist, as on a motorcycle, to accelerate the tank. Turning the yoke turns the tank much like a handlebar turns a motorcycle.

Although the M1 Abrams is relatively easy to drive compared to many other tanks, driving a tank should not be confused with driving the family automobile! Sixty tons of steel moving at forty miles per hour can do a tremendous amount of damage, not only to a hapless bit of real estate but to the tank itself. Running a tank into a dirt embankment at top speeds can rip off the front idler wheel and cause a serious accident.

Tanks are surprisingly maneuverable for their size and are able to pivot steer. This is sometimes described as neutral steering or turning on a dime, although in this case, it's a mighty big dime! During a pivot turn, the track on one side is propelled forward while the track on the other side is put in reverse. The tank turns around through a complete 360-degree circle without having to move either forward or back.

For the uninitiated, the strangest aspect of driving a tank is the lack of side and rear vision. The driver can see ahead fairly well, but the turret prevents any vision aft. When moving in reverse, the driver requires the assistance of the tank commander, or other members of the turret crew, to provide steering instructions.

TANK TRAINING

As weapons become more advanced, operating them becomes more expensive. Tank ammunition costs more than $500 a round. A set of tank tracks costs about $50,000 and they last a few thousand miles at best. But as historical examples suggest, a well-trained crew has a distinctive edge on the battlefield. How to train a tank crew while remaining within a tight budget is a real challenge.

Combat aircraft have had sophisticated simulators for training purposes for many years. Until the 1980s, most tank training was undertaken with simple mechanical trainers. These pipe-work skeletons vaguely resembled the crew compartments of a tank. Driver's simulators contained the same controls as the real tank, but the driver just stared ahead at the wall of the training building and pretended to drive off into realms unknown. Turret trainers contained the basic elements of the turret interior, and so were useful to familiarize the crew with the basic functions of the turret controls. But they didn't create a realistic environment in which the crew members could test their skills.

The advent of inexpensive computers in the 1980s permitted the development of extremely sophisticated trainers that more closely simulate reality. The new conduct-of-fire trainer (COFT) not only simulates the basic controls of an M1 tank but also provides the gunner with realistic computer targets to engage. This permits instructors to determine, without wasting expensive ammunition, how effectively their students are learning to operate the fire control systems. Driver trainers provide the student driver with realistic situations and test his reactions to them. These simulators are essentially a grown-up Nintendo—considerably more sophisticated but not unfamiliar in concept to anyone who has fed quarters into the better arcade games!

The real breakthrough is Simnet, being created at the U.S. Army's Armor Center at Fort Knox, Ken-

Tanker's hell—a thrown track. Few jobs are as disliked as repairing a track, especially if in soft soil.
Greg Stewart

tucky. The Simnet computers portray an imaginary battlefield with imaginary enemy tanks, infantry vehicles, and helicopters. What is remarkable about this system is that it can link the imaginary battlefield with several dozen individual tank simulators to fight mock battles. Previous simulators were useful in teaching basic skills, such as how to operate the laser range finder and how to work the brakes on a tank. Simnet offers an opportunity to train not only individual tank crews but entire tank battalions. It permits dozens of vehicles to interact in real time—a phenomenal development in training technology.

The tankers participating in an exercise enter a large hangarlike building attached to the main com-puter facility. The hangar is filled with row upon row of identical containers about the size of a family van. The containers display no hint of their contents but have several small doors on their sides. Each container is a replica of the interior of an M1 tank. The interiors are not intended to be true duplicates, and many details are simplified. But all the essential controls are there. The simulated tanks can be driven over the computer battlefield, engaging enemy tanks and vehicles as they do so. Care has to be taken in operating them, because on this battlefield, just as on a real battlefield, the computer tanks may be your own forces. (The first time the author ventured forth in a Simnet tank, he was put out of action almost

As in all army slots, sitting and waiting is part of the tanker's daily experience, even in the field. A tank *commander scans the horizon at the National Training Center.* Greg Stewart

immediately by a trigger-happy friendly tank.) Simnet will permit tank platoons and tank companies to train together to improve team interaction. The system will eventually be extended nationwide to allow tankers at Fort Hood, Texas, to fight with (or against) tankers at Fort Knox, Kentucky.

Backing up the Simnet is a recording and analysis center, which allows trainers to study the performance of the unit and suggest improvements. Simnet is also proving valuable in evaluating new weapons technologies. For example, the simulators can be modified with a new system, such as a new commander's sight, to see what impact this addition has on the performance of the crew in combat.

Improvements in tank training have extended much beyond the labs. A sterile environment such as Simnet is useful in teaching tankers the basic skills of tank combat, but real battle is a confusing mixture of noise, exhaustion, and chaos that is impossible even for today's best computers to duplicate. Exercises in the field still have a very important part to play in training.

One of the most useful innovations for field training has been the laser simulator. The U.S. Army uses a system called MILES (multiple integrated laser engagement system). When using the MILES system, a laser emitter is mounted in the tank's gun, which duplicates the tank gun firing. The tank is then fitted with strips of laser detectors—hit sensors—around

Household chores. Sweeping down a tank is not as useful as it might seem. Dust has a way of slipping into cracks and crevices of the tanks, jamming criti- *cal parts. George Patton was a fussy advocate of clean tanks, much to the chagrin of his young tankers.* Michael Green

the turret. Other weapons taking part in the mock battles are fitted with similar devices. However, M16 assault rifles send out a laser beam with a code different from that of a weapon such as a Dragon antitank missile. As a result, an M16 rifle can't knock out a tank.

The hit sensors on the tank are linked by an onboard system that determines whether the hit has killed the tank. A laser hit on the tank from a stray rifle shot is ignored, while a hit from a tank laser may be judged to have killed the tank. When a tank is killed, the MILES system automatically turns off the main gun's laser emitter to prevent it from firing. And the MILES system ignites a smoke grenade or flashing beacon to let the opponent know that he has been successful in hitting his target.

For American tankers in Germany, the tank heater seems to be a particular nesting ground for gremlins. Needless to say, tank heaters usually don't work in the cold winter months, and in the hot summer months, they become locked on and can't be turned off. Brian Gibbs

The MILES system permits a vast improvement in the conduct of extensive war games. Two opposing forces can engage each other in mock combat with realistic results. Prior to the development of MILES and its European counterparts, such as Simfire and Talissi, war games were little more than spectacles of military choreography. Tank units taking part were assigned predetermined roles and thus learned little from the results. Tank units engaged in war games with these new laser devices soon learn that if the enemy sees you, he is going to kill you. The field exercises drive home lessons that can be only vaguely understood from book learning and lectures.

The most elaborate of the war games using laser training techniques takes place at the National Training Center (NTC) at Fort Irwin, California. (The NTC experience is covered in detail in another book in this series, *NTC: A Primer of Modern Land Combat*, by Hans Halberstadt.) The NTC exercises are an army equivalent of the navy's Top Gun fighter exercises and the air force's Red Flag. It is an attempt to duplicate, as closely as possible in peacetime, the nature of real battlefield conditions. Computer simulators such as Simnet teach the basic skills of tank fighting; NTC puts those skills to the test.

One of the intriguing features of the NTC facility is its own resident opposing forces (OPFOR) units, which mimic Soviet-style mechanized formations. Although the units use some Warsaw Pact vehicles, most of their armored vehicles are Soviet look-alikes

Firing a tank gun also means having to clean out the tube later. It takes the whole crew to swab out the gun after a live-fire exercise. Michael Green

based on American vehicles. Surplus M-551 Sheridan tanks have been modified to resemble different Soviet vehicles, and these form the heart of the OPFOR tank force.

RUSSKIY TANKIST

The training and duty of an American tanker are very different from the experience of a Soviet tanker, or to use the Russian term, *tankist*. The Soviet army relies on draftees for its ground forces, unlike the U.S. Army, which is built around volunteer enlistments. As a result, American tankers are more experienced and better trained than their Soviet counterparts.

Draftees in the Soviet army serve a two-year tour of duty; there is virtually no reenlistment. The pay is lousy, the housing is spartan at best, and there is little risk that the food will ever rate a star in the Michelin guidebooks. The pay is only about twenty dollars a month, but there's not much to buy at base canteens anyway. Alcohol, including beer, is strictly forbidden for enlisted men, which is a real sacrifice for a Russian. Many recruits never have a chance to visit home during their two years of duty, and leave is seldom more than a chaperoned outing to a local town for a morally uplifting visit to a museum. Of course, most Soviet soldiers figure out how to smuggle a bit of moonshine onto the base and occasionally manage to become lost when on leave. But the life of a Soviet draftee has more in common with the life-style of a nineteenth-century soldier than with a member of today's American military.

Soviet tankers are more narrowly trained than their American counterparts. An American tanker will be cross-trained on all the positions in a tank. He will begin as a loader for some time, gradually earning his way from private to specialist fourth class, then moving to driver and eventually into the noncommissioned officer (NCO) ranks as a sergeant. It typically takes four years before an American soldier becomes a sergeant or has a chance to be a tank gunner or tank commander. In the Soviet army, there are few professional NCOs, so they have to fill the more advanced slots in the tank right away. Better recruits are selected shortly after induction for technical training as a tank commander. They are sent to an academy or a tank training regiment and are graduated as junior sergeants after a six-month course. The other members of the crew are usually sent straight to a tank regiment, or a tank training regiment, where they learn to drive a tank or operate the tank gun. They are seldom cross-trained in other roles.

As a result, Soviet tank crews are generally less experienced than their American counterparts. A typical U.S. tank has a sergeant, with several years' experience, serving as tank commander; a sergeant, with four years' experience, as gunner; a specialist fourth class, with a couple years' experience, as driver; and a private, with several months' experience, as loader. A typical Soviet tank crew might have a tank commander with a year and half of experience, a gunner with a year's duty, and a driver fresh out of technical training. Current Soviet tanks have an autoloader, so they do not have a fourth crewman.

Not only are Soviet tank crews apt to be younger and less experienced than American tank crews, they also receive less vigorous unit training and fewer live exercises. Compared to American training, a larger percentage of Soviet tank training is conducted using simulators, and these are usually of the older, more outdated type. This is due to the fact that Soviet tanks are generally less durable than NATO tanks and so are not used as much for training. There are restrictions on the number of hours any individual tank can be operated in one year, which is typically less than half the American average. Tank gunnery practice often uses subcaliber devices rather than live ammunition. On average, a Soviet tank crew fires less than ten rounds a year of main gun ammunition, compared to about a hundred rounds for American crews. The Soviets are trying to increase the amount of simulator training to cut down on operating costs. The current plan calls for a reduction in the number of actual tank rounds fired by a crew per year to only two.

As a result, Soviet gunnery skills tend to be poorer than those of their American counterparts. The Soviet training norm for engaging and destroying a target presumes that it will take thirty seconds for the tank commander to designate the target to the gunner and for the gunner to fire the first round. It is then assumed that the gunner will require two more rounds, taking fifteen seconds apiece, to have an 85 percent kill probability at normal combat ranges. This means a total of one minute to engage and destroy a hostile tank. During the Canadian Army Trophy meet, NATO teams typically took only ten to fifteen seconds to hit their targets, with a very high hit probability. Although these were Olympic-caliber crews, often with special training for the event, average crews are not that far behind.

The mediocre quality of Soviet tank training is symptomatic of the Soviet philosophy of war. The Soviets choose to overwhelm an opponent with a larger quantity of men and machines rather than outfight them on a one-to-one basis. Soviet tankers may be poorly trained, and their tanks may not perform as well, but in the event of a confrontation with NATO, they would have two or three tanks for every NATO tank. This is a philosophy borne out of the hard lessons of World War II. The Soviets view tank war as a brutal affair in which tanks (and their crews) are likely to survive only a few battles. They see no point in lavishing on their tanks fancy new features, such as thermal sights and three-axis stabilization systems.

Another ring in tanker's hell—a broken engine. Repairing tank engines often means using a crane to remove the whole powerpack. Brian Gibbs

And they see no point in spending thousands of rubles a year on professional soldiers when simple conscripts are adequate.

Operation Desert Storm strongly suggests that the Soviet approach to tank crew training is grossly inadequate. The Soviets have been quick to claim that Desert Storm proves nothing about either their equipment or their training procedures. But Iraqi tank crew training is far closer to Soviet practices than it is to American practices.

Although American military technology performed magnificently in Desert Storm, this can obscure the real source of the victory. Modern military technology requires extensive training and considerable crew skill for the machine to demonstrate its technical capabilities. American tankers in the Gulf War did enjoy significant technological advantages over their Iraqi opponents. But they held a more substantial advantage in crew quality. Even though there were many large scale tank-vs.-tank engagements, the Iraqis were seldom able to hit their opponents. This suggests a very poor level of basic crew skills. In contrast, American tank crews were able to engage Iraqi tanks at the outer edges of the weapon envelope where engagement is the most difficult, and consistently score hits.

It should also be remembered that not all American tank units enjoyed technological advantage over the Iraqis. The four Marine tank battalions with M60A1 tanks held no particular advantage over Iraqi units with T-62s or T-72s, yet the Marines had no particular difficulties overcoming Iraqi resistance.

Beyond the tactical shortcomings of the Iraqi tank force, they proved to be no match in tank operations. Iraqi divisional commanders were not able to employ their armor units in any significant fashion. Most Iraqi units fought from prepared positions, giving the initiative to American and other Allied units. This was in part due to overwhelming Allied air supremacy. But in cases where Allied air power was not present, for example, in the Iraqi attack on Khafji in January 1991, the Iraqis proved no more able to effectively wield tank forces on the battlefield.

The Khafji attack was a fiasco. The Iraqis intended the Khafji attack to be a major offensive by three mechanized divisions down the Saudi coast as a riposte to the Allied bombing campaign. In fact, of the three divisions, the Iraqis managed to launch only three brigades of one division in the attack. The other divisions did not manage to get their tank battalions rolling for twelve to twenty-four hours after the intended start time. As a result, the attack was uncoordinated and ineffective. The first wave of Iraqi tanks and infantry transporters was chopped to bits by a combined Saudi-Qatari armored force backed up by U.S. Marine artillery and helicopter gunships. By the time the remaining Iraqi tank battalions began to move, U.S. air power had been alerted. The Iraqi mobilization areas were soon swarming with A-10 Thunderbolt IIs and AV-8B Harriers, and hundreds of tanks and armored vehicles were lost.

TANK FORCE

Tank tactics have been the source of endless debate for the past half century. Ever since the first use of tanks in the muddy fields of the western front in World War I, tacticians have been arguing about what makes the most effective use of these weapons.

The key dilemma is how to use the tank in relation to the other combat arms, such as infantry and artillery. The integration of tanks, infantry, and artillery on the battlefield is usually referred to as combined arms tactics. Tanks are excellent assault weapons. They have protection to survive the blows of enemy defenses and mobility to break through enemy positions and attack the opponent's poorly protected command and supply echelons. But tanks are not good at holding onto terrain or clearing it of enemy troops. They are too few in number for such a purpose, for which infantry is much more effective. Nor are tanks good in all terrain. They are particularly ill suited to urban fighting, fighting in mountainous areas, and fighting in dense forests. In these cases, they can still be used to support the infantry, but the foot soldiers will bear the brunt of the fighting.

On a typical European battlefield, the terrain is mixed. Villages, towns, and woods break up a landscape of farm fields and open meadows. Villages and woods can conceal enemy antitank teams, making them effective barriers against tank action unless the tanks are supported by infantry and artillery. Tank tactics in World War I were fairly simple. Most of the early tanks were so slow that infantry could keep pace with them. By the outbreak of World War II, tanks had become much faster, typically operating at speeds of fifteen miles per hour or more. There was little consensus on how tank units should be structured and how they should be mixed with other combat arms. The issue of tank-infantry cooperation was particularly difficult.

The Germans were the most successful practitioners of tank tactics in the early years of World War II, fashioning an effective mixture of tanks, infantry, artillery, and close air support. The Germans would use a panzer division as the spearhead of an attack, backed by two or more infantry divisions. A panzer division typically had two hundred or more tanks and would have a regiment of mechanized infantry (*panzergrenadiers*) to support the tanks. The panzer-

The diesel engine of the M60A1 became quite familiar to most American tankers of the past two decades. Many older tankers remember it with some fondness, preferring it to the more modern turbine in the M1 Abrams. Brian Gibbs

grenadiers were carried in armored half-tracks, which gave them as much mobility as the tanks. Particularly stubborn resistance would be bludgeoned by fast, motorized artillery, or attacked from the air. In some operations, the panzer divisions would be concentrated into even larger formations, with several divisions working together as the spearhead for an attack stretched over a hundred miles or more of the battle line.

The German successes in Poland in 1939, France in 1940, and the Soviet Union in 1941 heavily influenced the American armored force. As in the German case, the American armored divisions were a blend of tank battalions, mechanized infantry on half-tracks, and self-propelled artillery. The remainder of the armored force was formed into separate tank battalions, used to support infantry divisions. The armored divisions were first used in combat in 1943 in North Africa and saw their most extensive combat duty in northwestern Europe following the June 1944 Normandy invasion. In theaters such as the Pacific, where the terrain was ill suited to large-scale mechanized

Tanker's hell revisited, this time with the added delight of mud. Fixing the track of an M60A1 tank in Germany. Brian Gibbs

operations, the separate tank battalions were used to provide close support to the infantry.

Today's armored units are an evolutionary outgrowth of the wartime formations. The U.S. Army currently fields four regular armored divisions and two National Guard armored divisions. Two of the armored divisions are stationed in Germany—the 3d Armored Division near Frankfurt and the 1st Armored Division near Nuremburg. The other two regular armored divisions, the 2d Armored Division and the 1st Cavalry Division, are located at Fort Hood, Texas. The two National Guard armored divisions are located in New Jersey (50th Armored) and in Texas (49th Armored). The armored divisions are the most concen-trated element of today's U.S. Army armored force, but there are many other armored units, including a number of armored brigades, as well as armored battalions, serving in mechanized infantry formations. In total, the U.S. Army has nearly a hundred tank battalions (numbering a bit more than fifty tanks each), with a little more than half being regular and the remainder National Guard. In the late 1980s, ten battalions (all National Guard) were equipped with the M48A5, about fifty battalions with the M60A1 or M60A3, and about forty with the M1, IPM1, or M1A1 Abrams tanks. A single battalion, the 3/73d Armor with the 82d Airborne Division, is still equipped with the air-portable M551A1 Sheridan tank. These num-

The tanker's world: dust, sun and diesel fumes.
Michael Green

108

bers are changing as more and more battalions convert to the Abrams tank. Eventually, about 7,000 Abrams tanks are expected to be added to army inventory.

The modernization of the armor battalions with the M1 Abrams has been accompanied by similar efforts in other elements of the armored division. The mechanized infantry battalions, equipped with the M113 armored personnel carrier (APC) since the early 1960s, are now being modernized with the M2 Bradley infantry fighting vehicle. The Bradley adds considerable firepower to the infantry squad, being equipped with a 25mm Bushmaster automatic cannon and a twin TOW antitank missile launcher. The Bradley was developed in response to the rapid growth of

the Warsaw Pact light armored vehicle inventory in the late 1960s and early 1970s. The M113 APC is armed with an unprotected .50-caliber machine gun, which is incapable of penetrating the thin armor of light armored vehicles, such as its Soviet counterpart, the BTR-60 armored transporter. In contrast, the Bradley's autocannon is fully protected and can knock out any armored vehicle short of a main battle tank. Its TOW missile launcher allows it to defend itself against main battle tanks. The Bradley also enjoys substantially better armor protection than the M113 APC. The M113 was designed to resist small arms ammunition, such as 7.62mm assault rifle fire. In contrast, the new M2A2 version of the Bradley can

Modern armored warfare is combined arms. The tanks work with mechanized infantry like these *riflemen with their M2 Bradley infantry fighting vehicle in the background.* Michael Green

withstand fire up to 30mm cannons, such as those fitted on the Soviet BMP-2 infantry fighting vehicle.

Like the M1 Abrams, the M2 Bradley has received a fair amount of press criticism. It has been widely derided as insufficiently armored, ignoring of course that it is the most thickly armored infantry vehicle in the world today. Although armies might like to buy armored infantry vehicles as heavily armored as main battle tanks, no army has the budget to do so. A heavy infantry vehicle would be about double the cost of the current Bradley. It's not simply the initial purchase cost that makes such heavy infantry vehicles impossible. Annual operating costs would be at least three times higher than those of the Bradley, due to the greater stress placed on the track, suspension, and power plant by heavier weight.

Infantry vehicles such as the Bradley are expected to support the tank in combined arms operations. This does not mean that they literally fight side by side; rather, a Bradley mechanized infantry battalion might be used in support of an M1 Abrams battalion. The M1 battalion would pave the way for the attack, because its better protection permits it to survive enemy antitank missiles and gunfire better than the Bradley. The Bradley would work in conjunction with the M1 Abrams but some distance behind. Its autocannon can accurately hit targets more than a mile away, and its TOW missiles have an even greater reach. It should not be forgotten that the Bradley's main function is to transport its infantry squad. In close terrain, such as woods and urban areas, dismounted infantry supported by armor is more efficient than tanks alone.

The Bradley is also widely used in the U.S. Army as a scout vehicle, serving in armored cavalry formations. In this role, the M3 Bradley cavalry fighting vehicle does not carry an infantry squad in the rear compartment, as does its stablemate, the M2 infantry fighting vehicle. The role of an armored cavalry forma-tion is to seek out the enemy. Once the enemy is found, it can be attacked by the main force, be it tanks, mechanized infantry, artillery, or aircraft.

One of the most obvious changes in U.S. armored divisions since World War II has been the considerable expansion of army aviation. Armored and mechanized infantry divisions now have their own helicopter units, used for scouting, troop transport, and close air support. The UH-60 Blackhawk helicopter is an airborne equivalent of the M2 Bradley infantry vehicle, transporting troops rapidly by air. The AH-64 Apache attack helicopter can provide close air support for mechanized units, using its 30mm cannon, rockets, or laser-guided Hellfire antitank missiles.

Desert Storm was a clear display of these combined arms tactics. The attack on the ground was preceded by nearly forty days of pulverizing air attacks. On the eve of the ground offensive, the forward Iraqi positions were pummeled again by artillery. Iraqi border defenses were surmounted by a careful operation of combat engineer troops, followed by dismounted infantry to secure the breach. The tank forces followed only after the breach had been secured. But once the initial layers of defensive barriers were surmounted, the tank and mechanized infantry formations were able to pour into Iraq at breakneck speeds, out-pacing the ability of the Iraqi forces to react.

The Gulf War showed the increasing role played by attack helicopters in modern tank warfare. Army AH-64 Apache and Marine AH-1W Super Cobra helicopters fired about 5,000 Hellfires missiles during the course of the war, the majority destroying their target. The Apaches proved to be a critical ingredient in the rapid advances of U.S. Army maneuver units. The growing role of attack helicopters in mobile warfare may be one of the critical lessons of the Gulf War.

Chapter 6

Twenty-First-Century Tank

This book began by quoting the mistaken prophecy that "tanks have no future." So it's appropriate to end by taking a look at tanks over the next decade, into the twenty-first century.

At the moment, the most exotic area of development is in the future tank cannon. With continuing advances in tank armor, current tank guns are likely to become inadequate over the next decade. Tank

It will be a decade at least before a successor to the M1A1 Abrams appears. In the meantime, the U.S. Army will also be looking at whether to replace the old M–551 Sheridan with a more modern vehicle. Greg Stewart

111

gun size has escalated steadily since World War II, paralleling the ever-increasing effectiveness of tank armor. Tank guns in 1945 were typically 75mm; by 1960 they were 105mm and today they are 120mm. Boosting tank gun size any further has serious drawbacks. To begin with, bigger guns inevitably mean a larger ammunition round than is in use today. This is bad for two reasons. First, fewer rounds of ammunition can be carried. Second, a greater internal volume in the vehicle hull is likely to be filled with ammuni-

tion propellant—a nasty fire hazard, as we have seen earlier.

The decline in the number of rounds of ammunition has been a steady trend. Tanks with 105mm guns typically carried sixty-five rounds, whereas tanks with 120mm guns typically carry forty. Forty rounds may seem like a lot, but American tankers in World War II complained that they ran out of ammunition too quickly. And they carried eighty-five rounds in their M-4 Sherman tanks! The Israelis found that ammuni-

Besides being used by the 82nd Airborne Division, the Sheridan has soldiered on at the National Training center, being used primarily by the OPFOR units as a Vismod—a visually modified vehicle imitating Soviet vehicle types. Michael Green

tion use in battle was far higher than expected, and, worst of all, replenishment was a difficult feat to accomplish on a contemporary, highly lethal battlefield. Ammunition had to be brought forward in unprotected trucks and then laboriously loaded, round by round, through the narrow roof hatch of the tank. The Israelis adopted an ingenious pallet, containing a few dozen rounds of ammunition, for rapidly reloading their Merkava tank. It doesn't entirely solve the problem, but it helped.

In the short term, these problems are unlikely to be completely solved. A future gun, currently being developed by NATO, will probably be used on the new tanks of 1999: the American Block 3* tank and the German Panzer 2000. It is likely to be a 140mm gun, similar in technology to today's guns. The ammunition storage problems will probably be lessened by adopting autoloaders.

The first main battle tank outside the Soviet bloc to receive an autoloader will be France's new AMX Leclerc tank. The French began their new tank program almost a decade after the M1 and Leopard II generation but a generation before the Block 3 and the Panzer 2000. Therefore, it has features that straddle the current and future generations. Autoloaders are attractive for a variety of reasons. They take up less space than a human loader, so the tank can be smaller and lighter, or they can stow more ammunition. They are more effective than a human loader when the tank is moving at high cross-country speeds. As we saw earlier, loading a tank gun while moving cross-country is a tricky business. The drawback of autoloaders is that they reduce the crew to only three men. Tank forces with combat experience, such as the Israelis, feel that three men are too few to keep a tank functional in battlefield conditions. Time and experience will tell. Perhaps some rethinking of maintenance procedures will help solve the problem. But autoloaders and three-man crews do seem to be the wave of the future.

Another way around the ammunition problem has been suggested by Swedish designers, who came up with a conceptual design for a new tank called MBT 2000. It is armed with a new 140mm gun, with only about twenty-five rounds of ammunition—too few rounds to most tankers' tastes! But alongside the 140mm gun is a smaller 40mm automatic cannon with two hundred rounds of 40mm ammunition. It is often forgotten that tank guns are not used primarily for fighting other tanks. Typically, two-thirds of tank ammunition is high-explosive rounds, used to attack "soft" targets, such as light armored vehicles, trucks, and buildings. The Swedish idea is to mount the big gun exclusively for the "hard" targets, such as enemy tanks, and a smaller gun for soft targets. Nearly a dozen rounds of 40mm ammunition can be carried for every round of 140mm, and a dozen rounds of 40mm are more than a match for one round of 140mm against most of these targets. The U.S. Army had considered a similar approach back in the 1970s with the XM-1, planning to mount a 25mm Bushmaster cannon next to the 105mm gun. The idea was dropped due to problems found at the time with the Bushmaster gun. This approach may be revived in the U.S. or Europe and may help solve the ammunition storage problem in the short run.

In the long run, however, conventional guns will be replaced by novel gun technologies now under development. Three new types of guns are being studied: liquid propellant guns (LPG), electrothermal guns (ETG), and electromagnetic force guns (EMF). All have distinct advantages over current guns, but it has yet to be seen which will prove practical.

Liquid propellant guns are an idea that has been around for a long time. Instead of having dozens of large and awkward casings full of powder propellant, which are difficult for the loader to handle, why not put the propellant in a single big tank and pump it into the gun like fuel? The first experiments with LPG weapons began in the 1950s. These were called bulk-loaded guns. The problem was that consistent detonation of the propellant was tricky, so the guns weren't as accurate as conventional guns. In the late 1970s, companies such as General Electric Aerospace developed a new concept called regenerative injection LPG, which uses a more sophisticated breech mechanism to load and fire the gun. This was first explored for use on self-propelled artillery systems, but in the past few years, serious attention has been paid to using this technology for tank guns.

There are several reasons why these guns promise to be superior to conventional guns. One of the main technical attractions is that the detonation of the propellant can be controlled to shape the duration and levels of bore pressure. What this means in simple English is that the guns push a projectile out of the tube at a higher speed, thereby gaining better penetration of the enemy tank's armor. The other attractive feature of LPG technology is that it aids tank survivability. The propellant being used in these tests is a variety of ammonium nitrate, chemically similar to

liquid fertilizer. An unpleasant smell no doubt, but without the fire hazard of current solid propellants. In addition, a tank using a liquid propellant gun could even store the propellant outside the main armor of the tank, since it needs only a small hole to be pumped into the gun. The storage of liquid propellants could better exploit small cavities in the tank's design, allowing the tank to carry more ammunition.

The main drawback of LPG weapons is that a new tank will have to be built around them. They probably can't be retrofitted to existing tanks without extensive rebuilding. A new technology that has retrofit potential, as well as many of the other advantages

FMC Corporation, makers of the Bradley infantry fighting vehicle, offered the Army a light tank based on Bradley components which they called the XM4

AGS. The Army desires a light tank that could be easily airlifted to hot spots like Grenada or Panama. Huck Hagenbuch/FMC Corp.

114

Teledyne Continental, best known for their tank engines, developed this light tank design in the 1980s. It uses an elevated, external gun in place of a turret to keep vehicle weight low. Teledyne Continental

of LPG weapons, is the electrothermal gun. The electrothermal gun uses ammunition that closely resembles today's tank ammunition. The liquid propellant is stored in a metal cartridge casing at the base of the projectile in a fashion not much different from today's tank ammunition. There are two key differences. First, the new propellant is not flammable by itself; in fact, it is even less energetic under ordinary conditions than the liquid propellant of the LPG weapon. Second, the casing has a small electrical anode at the base. The electrothermal gun, when fired, passes a controlled electrical charge into the propellant, which detonates the material. As in an LPG weapon, the ignition method allows the detonation to be controlled, giving the gun better performance than today's solid propellant guns. There are several different ETG concepts being studied today. The FMC Corporation's combustion-augmented plasma (CAP) gun is suitable for tanks as well as warships and artillery. General Dynamics is exploring an electrothermal launch system originally developed for the Strategic Defense Initiative Star Wars program.

It seems very likely that tanks in the early twenty-first century will use some form of liquid propellant gun or electrothermal gun, although neither technology is fully proven and decisions regarding which system is more effective probably won't be possible until the mid- or late 1990s. Even more exotic than these weapons are the EMF, or electromagnetic force, guns, which may appear a decade or more after these other types of guns. The EMF guns are another offshoot of Star Wars. They have no propellant at all in the usual sense of the word. Their action depends entirely on electrical energy. An electrical generator is used to create a strong electromagnetic field that "repels" the projectile at tremendous velocities. Current tank guns fire their projectiles at speeds of about 1.8 kilometers per second. The EMF guns have fired projectiles at 10 kilometers per second. These projectiles were actually more similar to hockey pucks than to antitank projectiles. But at such high velocities, they can cut through amazing amounts of steel.

The EMF guns are unlikely to prove practical as tank weapons for at least a decade. The current systems use massive electrical capacitors to store the enormous amounts of electrical energy needed to fire a projectile. These are so large that it would require one vehicle to mount the gun and another to mount the power supply. In addition, the early systems can be fired only a single time before many key components have to be rebuilt—hardly practical for a conventional weapon! The EMF guns will follow electrothermal and liquid propellant guns, if they ever do prove practical.

Advances in gun technology have led to studies of new antitank projectile designs. Novel gun technologies create a whole new set of challenges. As projectile speeds start reaching the 2.5- to 3-kilometer-per-second threshold, difficulties begin to appear. At these speeds, the projectiles are flying nearly as fast as meteorites entering the earth's atmosphere. And as with meteorites, the temperatures caused by air friction become so high that portions of the projectiles can actually be burned away.

Armor technology is likely to proceed apace, trying to protect against these new weapons. This area is highly classified, so it's hard to predict what directions might be taken. Some information has leaked out about a new concept called electromagnetic armor. This would apparently work like reactive armor, but instead of using the chemical energy of explosives to hurl a disrupting plate at the projectile, the armor would use electromagnetic energy. So far, no clear explanation has appeared on how such a system would function.

One of the main challenges in tank protection in the 1990s will be protection against top attack. Until now, most of the antitank weapons have been directed against the front and sides of tanks. But as the front and side armor has gotten thicker and thicker, antitank missile designers have come to realize that other approaches are necessary. The top armor of tanks is very thin, since up to now the only threat has been overhead artillery airbursts.

In the mid-1980s, the Swedish army introduced the Bill missile, a medium infantry antitank missile about the size of the Euromissile Milan. But instead of detonating against the front of the tank, the missile is programmed to fly about three feet over the tank. As it passes over the center of the tank, it fires its shaped-charge warhead down into the roof. Modified versions of existing NATO missiles that are entering service in the early 1990s, such as the British FITOW (future improved TOW) and the American TOW-2B, use a similar approach. And nearly all of the new generation of antitank missiles, e.g., the American AAWS-M and the European Trigat-MR, also use top attack. To make matters worse, new artillery-fired munitions, such as SADARM (sense and destroy anti-armor munition), also attack the thinly protected roofs of tanks.

These weapons are no different from other weapons in the way they penetrate armor. The problem in protecting against this new threat is that tanks are

The FMC XM-4 AGS combines the firepower of a main battle tank in a chassis less than half the weight. The weight savings comes from smaller ve-hicle size and substantially less armor. Huck Hagenbuch/FMC Corp.

already near the limit of their weight. If tanks grow any heavier than seventy tons, it becomes extremely difficult to drive them across normal bridges, transport them in existing ships or transport aircraft, and move them with existing tank transporters and rail flatcars. To add enough armor to the large roof area of a tank would add too much weight. There is some hope that new generations of advanced reactive armor may be the solution. But the matter of roof protection will be one of the trickiest problems confronting tank designers in the 1990s.

Rapid advances in tank fire controls are likely to continue into the next century. One of the most ambitious efforts now being explored is the addition of a millimeter wave (mm wave) radar to the existing thermal sights carried on tanks. A mm wave radar system

The Army has been reluctant to call these futuristic vehicles tanks. They have the firepower and mobility of tanks, but not the armor protection. They prefer instead to call them armored gun systems (AGS) or other such euphemisms. Teledyne Continental

has certain advantages over thermal sights. It has better range than thermal imaging sights and it can "see" in circumstances where the thermal sight cannot, for example, when smoke grenades are used that blind thermal sights. A mm wave radar system has other attractive features: for example, it may be possible, for the first time, to link the sensors with a computer and for the computer to identify the target.

Target identification has always been a problem on the battlefield. Tanks in combat are usually encumbered with camouflage nets, crew gear, and other objects that obscure their shapes. When looking through his sights, a tank gunner must wonder, Is that a friendly Leopard II or is it an unfriendly T-72? Often, it's hard to tell until the tanks are quite close. To best take advantage of the long-range fire-

The elevated, external gun configuration on the Teledyne Continental vehicle is also being examined for future main battle tanks. One of the main drawbacks is that it places the tank commander low *in the hull where it is difficult to carry out his traditional mission of surveillance of the surrounding terrain.* Teledyne Continental

power of modern tank guns, it is becoming necessary to investigate new ways to identify tanks accurately as friend or foe. Advances in millimeter wave radar promise to make this possible.

These new technologies have a synergistic effect, to use a term now in vogue with the high-tech crowd. That is to say, two new technologies complement each other so effectively that the end performance is much greater than would be expected from adding the two systems together. The mm wave radar and autoloader are good examples. A computer-sensor link will make target identification much quicker, and autoloading will allow the tank gun to fire more often. Tanks of the M-60A1 generation could be realistically expected to engage one or two targets a minute. Tanks of the next generation might be able to engage six per minute.

Future tanks are likely to communicate with one another in a fashion very different from that of today. Until now, tanks have communicated by radio, which is still perfectly adequate, but radio can be intercepted by the enemy, or jammed. New tanks, such as the French AMX Leclerc and the improved American M1A2, are being built around integrated digital electronic architectures. They will have new data handling systems that permit more than simple voice messages to be transmitted. For example, a battalion commander might wish to let his tank platoon commanders know where neighboring friendly units are located, and where scout helicopters have located an enemy tank formation. Communicating this information over the radio would be risky, since, if intercepted, it would expose the locations of friendly forces and warn the enemy that his forces had been detected. With the new systems, the data can be burst-transmitted in code. The burst transmission compresses all the data into a microsecond signal and sends it at moments when the enemy is not jamming. The data is coded, to prevent the enemy from reading it, and is reinterpreted by the data handling system on the tank. It can be used to provide voice messages, but it can provide visual data as well. Future tank commanders will have small graphics displays in their tanks. Communications such as the one suggested could be transmitted as maps, showing enemy and friendly locations in a detailed fashion that would be impractical if transmitted by voice.

Advanced data handling systems, such as that on the AMX Leclerc, go one step further. The system links all the major sensors on the tank. It can then transmit this data to headquarters when the need arises. For example, the tank can continually transmit information, such as how many rounds of ammunition are left, how much fuel remains, and where the tank is located. The headquarters can then plan when to send forward additional fuel and ammunition supplies.

The future battlefield is likely to become dangerous in ways not imagined a decade ago. One of the most likely future menaces will be directed-energy weapons, the first of which will probably be the laser. Lasers are already used for a number of missions, e.g., as range finders. The current generation of lasers using neodymium/YAG (the type of material used in the lasing crystal) is not eye safe, that is, if the lasers hit the eye directly, they can cause damage. This is not intentional; laser range finders in tanks can be fired only in very short bursts and too infrequently to make them an effective weapon. Another common use for lasers on the battlefield is the laser target designator. These are aimed at a target, and then laser homing munitions (such as aircraft-carried laser homing bombs) steer themselves toward the reflections of laser light off the target.

Future laser weapons may be designed to actually damage soldiers or weapons, not simply guide other weapons. The first type likely to be deployed is an antisensor laser. As we have seen in this book, modern weapons sensors, such as thermal sights, are becoming increasingly important in modern tank combat. These

Next page
The question of the future of light tanks was partly clarified by the Gulf War: there are many Third World conflicts where nothing less than a main battle tank will do. The question is, are there other conflicts where a lighter, smaller, more compact tank would be adequate? Huck Hagenbuch/FMC Corp.

sensors, as well as conventional optical devices such as telescopic sights, are vulnerable to bursts of laser energy. Lasers can even damage aircraft canopies—certain types of lasers can cause Plexiglas to lose its transparency and turn opaque.

An antisensor laser uses a low-powered beam to scan the battlefield. When the beam comes in contact with a reflective surface, such as the glass or Plexiglas in a tank sight, the main laser fires a burst of medium-energy laser light, which damages the sight's delicate electrooptics, or opaques the glass or Plexiglas cover. This may seem farfetched, but the U.S. Army has already tested such a system, mounted on the Bradley infantry vehicle; called Stingray, it could be in service by 1992.

Such laser systems do not pose much danger to human eyesight, due to the low energy levels. But laser weapons capable of blinding tank crews and other troops are possible with current technology. As a result, new tank designs are beginning to incorporate filtration systems to prevent laser damage. It is much easier to protect troops in armored vehicles than out in the open. This is yet another reason why armored vehicles will remain a vital element in all future land armies.

As this book was being written, important changes were taking place in Central Europe that suggest a lessening of tensions between the Warsaw Pact and NATO countries. Indeed, by the early 1990s, there will probably be extensive conventional arms control reductions as a result. The pace of tank development will certainly be affected by these momentous events. A reduced threat of conventional war in Europe reduces the pressure for tank modernization. The super-power confrontation has been the main force driving continued tank development since the end of World

The main market for light tanks has traditionally been the Third World. Past U.S. Army experience with light tanks has not been entirely favorable since they are often mistakenly used in combat in place of main battle tanks instead of in their intended cavalry or tank destroyer roles. Huck Hagenbuch/FMC Corp.

War II. Arms reductions will slow the pace of development but are unlikely to result in the elimination of the main battle tank from Europe's armies.

The impact of the changes occurring in Europe may have other effects on U.S. Army tanks. There is likely to be a renewed interest in lighter tanks, which are more suitable for rapid deployment in brushfire wars in Third World countries. Tanks designed for the European theater, such as the M1A1 Abrams, are heavy and bulky; they are difficult to transport by sea and air. When the U.S. intervened in Panama in 1989, the troops were supported by M551 Sheridan light tanks that could be easily airlifted to the crisis area, but the Sheridan is due for retirement due to its age. The first American tanks to arrive in Saudi Arabia in August 1990 were 82nd Airborne's Sheridans. In the mid-1980s the army considered developing a light tank called the XM4 AGS (armored gun system). It led to some unique designs by Teledyne Continental and the FMC Corporation, but the program was scuttled due to its low priority. With the changing priorities in national strategy, this program may be revived.

Whether a new rapidly deployable tank will appear in the 1990s is unclear. What the U.S. Army's tank force will remain centered around is the more traditional main battle tank, and its battlefield companion, the infantry fighting vehicle. Michael Green

Light tanks offer firepower similar to that of main battle tanks but with substantially less armor. They are acceptable where the principal requirement is to rapidly insert a force to carry out a special mission, especially in situations where tanks and sophisticated antitank weapons are unlikely to be encountered. This covers Third World scenarios such as Grenada and Panama. But light tanks are not suitable in all Third World contingencies. Light tanks were not effective in Korea in 1950 or in Vietnam. During the Korean War, enemy tanks were a major threat. In Vietnam, antitank weapons such as the RPG-7 rocket launcher were numerous and used with deadly effect against light tanks and armored vehicles. Today, antitank rockets are even more widespread and are used by nearly every army and guerrilla group in the Third World. The RPG-7 may not be effective against main battle tanks in a major European war, but it is ideally suited for combatting light armor in a guerrilla war. The Soviets learned this lesson the hard way. The roads of Afghanistan are littered with the wrecks of hundreds of Soviet light armored vehicles, blown apart by antitank rockets and mines.

The advent of reactive armor may make the light tank more viable in Third World situations. Typically, antitank rockets, not antitank guns, have been the main weapon in these wars. It may prove possible to design a thirty-ton tank with advanced armor that could stop a typical antitank rocket's shaped-charge warhead. However, such a configuration would still be vulnerable to tank gun fire, unlike a main battle tank, which is protected against both antitank threats. Because of their vulnerability to tank guns, light tanks are less versatile than main battle tanks. They are useful in limited circumstances where there is a premium on transportability. But they are not particularly effective when combat survivability is important, as in much of the Third World today, where even small armies are well equipped with first-rate tanks.

Desert Storm serves as an important reminder that deployability of tanks should not take precedence over their combat survivability. There have been those who have argued that the United States should begin to field a new tank light enough to be airlifted into trouble

The tank may seem an archaic dinosaur in an age of missiles. But somehow, the tank has managed to continue to evolve to vanquish most of its erstwhile opponents. Greg Stewart

spots more easily than the massive M1A1 Abrams. Such a tank poses two problems. On the one hand, it creates the false impression to national policy makers that a heavy armored force can actually be rapidly deployed, when in fact, such a light armored force has distinct limitations if facing a real heavy armored force. As many paratroopers remarked, only half in jest when they were deployed to Saudi Arabia in 1990, they were there mainly as "speed bumps" to slow down any Iraqi attack into Saudi Arabia.

Light, rapidly deployable tanks are speed bumps when faced with real main battle tanks. This was obvious in 1950 when the U.S. Army tried to use M-24 tanks against Korean T-34s and when the Israelis tried to use AMX-13 tanks against T-34s and T-54s in 1967. They certainly have their utility in theaters where there is little or no armor present such as Grenada or Panama. But they do not have a significant role to play in much of the Third World where large tank forces are becoming increasingly common.

If in the future American forces are to be deployed in land warfare in distant regions of the Third World, the policy planners should first address the issue of whether such forces can be deployed with needed armored and mechanized forces. The issue should not be about tailoring the American forces with speed bump tanks to make such deployments easier.

The U.S. Army may adopt a light tank to replace the aging M551 Sheridan later in the 1990s, but such a vehicle remains marginal to armored warfare. It is a valuable weapon in combat contingencies when enemy armored forces are small or nonexistent. It should have no place being committed against forces with contemporary main battle tanks.

There have been some arms-control schemes put forward that would eliminate tanks entirely. These are based on the dubious notion that tanks are "offensive" weapons. The sophomoric categorization of weapons into "defensive" and "offensive" arms is popular in academic circles but is a meaningless concept in the face of battlefield realities. Offensive weapons are seen as increasing the likelihood of war, and the tank is seen as a prime culprit, since it is mistakenly equated with modern maneuver warfare. Wars are not made more or less likely by the configuration of armies. The roots of war lie elsewhere, in the political world of international relations. Tinkering with the configuration of modern armies might make the horrors of trench war possible again, but it is unlikely to have much impact on the probability of conflict in Europe. Major Doug MacGregor, an armor officer with the 2d Armored Cavalry, concluded:

The tank remains today, as it has for several years, the most survivable piece of equipment on the battlefield. It has sufficient protection to allow it to survive against most artillery attacks, particularly if you are on the move. So for that reason, survivability, there is no alternative to the tank right now. The second reason is that it is probably the only piece of equipment that allows you to sustain your mobility, which is absolutely essential to offensive operations. What do you turn to if you don't have a tank? The tank is what allows you to carry the battle to the enemy. It allows you to move and close with him, and ultimately, to destroy him. There's nothing else on the battlefield that allows you to do that.

Tanks have remained the centerpiece of modern armies because of their versatility. They provide combat forces with capabilities that no other single weapon can offer. The many premature announcements of the demise of the tank highlight the remarkable resiliency of the main battle tank. Although new developments in antitank technology, e.g., top-attack missiles, will continue to challenge the tank's efficiency on the battlefield, concurrent advances in tank technology will raise questions about the value of antiarmor weapons. Futuristic tank design efforts with electrothermal guns, electromagnetic armor, and mm wave sensors may alter the appearance of tanks, but the role of the tank at the cutting edge of modern land forces will endure into the next century.

Index

About the Authors

Steven Zaloga holds a master's degree in East European history. He is the author of over thirty books on military technology and on the Soviet armed forces, including *Red Thrust: Attack on the Central Front, Soviet Tactics and Capabilities in the 1990s*. He has written numerous articles on military technology, including a monthly column on Soviet military affairs for *Armed Forces Journal International*. He is on the editorial board of *The Journal of Soviet Military Studies* and is a regular contributor to *Jane's Soviet Intelligence Review*. He is the writer and producer of a series of television documentaries on Desert Shield and Desert Storm for Video Ordnance, and was in Saudi Arabia in 1990 filming and photographing U.S. forces there for these programs. Zaloga lives in Connecticut.

Michael Green is a freelance photographer and writer specializing in defense matters. Besides writing for a wide range of domestic and foreign magazines, Green has coauthored a number of military photobooks published in England, Japan, and Hong Kong.